THE HEALING
SOURCE BOOK

DISCOVER YOUR OWN PATH TO
BETTER HEALTH AND INNER PEACE

David F Vennells

D1270526

Winchester, UK
Washington, USA)

First published by O Books, 2007
O Books is an imprint of John Hunt Publishing Ltd.,
The Bothy, Deershot Lodge, Park Lane, Ropley, Hants, SO24 0BE, UK
office1@o-books.net
www.o-books.net

Distribution in:

UK and Europe
Orca Book Services
orders@orcabookservices.co.uk
Tel: 01202 665432 Fax: 01202 666219 Int. code (44)

USA and Canada
NBN
custserv@nbnbooks.com
Tel: 1 800 462 6420 Fax: 1 800 338 4550

Australia and New Zealand
Brumby Books
sales@brumbybooks.com.au
Tel: 61 3 9761 5535 Fax: 61 3 9761 7095

Far East (offices in Singapore, Thailand, Hong Kong, Taiwan)
Pansing Distribution Pte Ltd
kemal@pansing.com
Tel: 65 6319 9939 Fax: 65 6462 5761

South Africa
Alternative Books
altbook@peterhyde.co.za
Tel: 021 447 5300 Fax: 021 447 1430

Text copyright David Vennells 2007

Design: Stuart Davies

ISBN-13: 978 1 846940 05 7
ISBN-10: 1 84694 005 2

A CIP catalogue record for this book is available from the British Library.

Printed in the US by Maple Vail

THE HEALING SOURCE BOOK

DISCOVER YOUR OWN PATH TO
BETTER HEALTH AND INNER PEACE

David F Vennells

BOOKS

Winchester, UK
Washington, USA

ACKNOWLEDGEMENTS

Many thanks to everyone who has contributed to the making of this book.

Special thanks to the following websites, all excellent online information, advice and product sources:

www.aworldofaromatherapy.com
www.abc-of-yoga.com
www.aromaweb.com
www.yogabasics.com
www.mindstones.com
www.homeopathic.org
www.abchomeopathy.com
www.herbalremediesinfo.com
www.aworldofchinesemedicine.com

For more information on other books by the same author visit
www.healingbooks.co.uk

CONTENTS

INTRODUCTION

This book is designed to provide you with all the practical complementary healing techniques and ideas that can be safely and successfully practiced without expert tuition. Each chapter teaches the essential techniques of a particular therapy or healing philosophy that can be easily learnt through following the simple instructions. You can develop your own healing plan without needing to consult qualified therapists or attend a college course. In terms of healing philosophies I particularly find the Buddhist approach to be very practical, inspirational and effective, so I have also included a little of this timeless wisdom in the hope that it will provoke some contemplation of the real meaning of health and healing.

I became interested in complementary therapies during a long term illness. After suffering from Chronic Fatigue Syndrome for many years a friend suggested I try an alternative approach. I was not interested in natural medicine at the time, but this simple suggestion opened up a new world to me. The natural approach to healing looks at the whole person and addresses the deeper causes of illness rather than just the symptoms. Understanding natural medicine is really about understanding human nature. I found some therapies to be so helpful to my physical, mental and spiritual wellbeing that I decided to train in these fields and try to help others gain similar benefit. This book is the culmination of 15 years of illness, searching and healing.

All deep, long lasting healing comes from healing the heart. Illness can often result from having and holding negative thoughts and feelings and healing can often result from simply transforming our negative minds into positive minds. To have a healthy heart means to have a sense of inner peace, to be at peace with ourselves and the world around us and particularly to have a mind of unconditional love towards others. If we have a strong sense of love in our heart it is difficult to be unhappy whether we are healthy or not! Establishing an experience of inner peace and love in our mind is a large part of the healing process.

So if we want to become a successful healer we need to learn the physical skills required but we also need to learn how to heal our own heart, then we can help others do the same. I hope this book is successful in teaching you both practical healing skills and some ways to improve your quality of life by improving the quality of your mind. Without an ongoing process of inner development no matter how good our technical skills become our healing will always be superficial.

The practical techniques in this book are not difficult to learn, all you need is enthusiasm and lots of people to practice on! You can practice on yourself or family and friends. All the techniques work well together and all are safe to use. You can begin practicing from day one as you read the book, indeed this is the best way to learn. There is no substitute for experience so the sooner you get started the sooner you will be able to use your new skills to help yourself and others. Enthusiasm, commitment and love guarantee success.

To get the most from this book use it to develop a healing plan, for yourself or others, that incorporates time each week for the therapies that feel right for your situation or for the people you are treating. For example, you could have a reflexology treatment once a week as well as an aromatherapy treatment and also practice a little yoga every day, take herbal and homeopathic remedies and do some meditation. If you develop a sustainable, gentle and enjoyable healing plan like this your health will definitely benefit from your new lifestyle.

Take a realistic long term approach; our body and mind needs time to heal, it can't happen in just a few weeks. So develop something like a three month plan and approach your healing from different angles. Use the natural healing techniques explained in this book, particularly concentrating on the ones that seem to work best for you or those that instinctively feel right. Also develop a good diet, do gentle exercise, drink plenty of water and most importantly try to develop a relaxed and positive approach to life.

If you are treating others take the same approach, sit down with them and talk about the idea of developing a realistic healing plan. Try to get a feel for where they are in terms of their health and how much can realistically be achieved over the following weeks and months. What do they want to achieve? What do they think is possible? What do they think is realistic? Don't ever give false or unrealistic hope, but always stay open to their potential for healing.

Finally there is always a right and a wrong time for healing and if you listen carefully to a patient and develop your intuition you will begin to feel what is happening and be able to help the patient make the most of their situation. Human life is about inner growth, so this is the most important aspect of complementary medicine. We would all love to have good health but this is not always what we need in order to become more complete human beings. The healer's real job is to help facilitate inner growth, not necessarily by giving advice which might often be misguided, but just by being there and being a living example of the true meaning of 'good health'. Good health is really just a state of mind, so we have to work on ourselves before we can really become an effective 'healer'. Having said that, just be natural, be yourself, don't take things too seriously, we can still just visit a friend and give them a massage and have a chat without feeling that we have to be a 'healer' all the time. Just being a normal, kind, patient and friendly person is very special; this is how we will heal our world.

1
PRINCIPLES OF NATURAL HEALING

Our body is an intricate web of interconnected physiological systems all dependent on each other. If one area is damaged or put under stress this can cause problems in other areas. Our body is like a microcosm of our planet. We are only just beginning to understand how well balanced the ecology of our planet was before mankind began to influence it. When one part of this delicate natural machine is disturbed it sends ripples of stress through the whole. If this disturbance is stopped then the whole is strong enough to rebalance but if this disturbance becomes stronger and continues for a long time then there comes a point where the world will never be able to recover. This is the same with our body, when we are healthy there is a delicate balance, all the systems of our body are working in harmony and we are mentally, emotionally and spiritually fulfilled. However if one area is persistently disturbed there is no doubt that this will adversely affect the whole and eventually we will get to a point of no return. So it is important to identify if something in our life is not balanced, maybe this is the cause or moreover the condition which has encouraged illness to develop. We will look more deeply at the actual causes of illness in a later chapter.

One of the most important aspects of natural healing is to understand that healing depends on balance. If our external and internal lifestyles are balanced then, assuming we have the potential to get well, all the conditions necessary for healing are in place. It is easy to understand how to establish external balance. We should develop a good diet, often just simple healthy food is best, drink plenty of water, get enough rest and sleep, have some regular exercise within our capacity and we need to have an enjoyable job or purpose in life or learn to enjoy it! Also it helps to live in a clean and healthy environment although not necessarily luxurious; we also need supportive and healthy relationships and should avoid excessive alcohol, smoking or drugs. These are encouraging external conditions that will support the healing process. If we cannot completely obtain the best external conditions we should do everything we can to move our life in that direction, definitely if we put our mind to it we can make some significant improvements. Good internal conditions are a little more difficult to understand. We will look more at this in the next chapter but for now we can say that we also need to learn how to balance and develop our inner qualities on a mental, emotional and spiritual level.

As well as a complex physical body we also have a subtle body made of 'energy'. This subtle body is made up of life force energy which runs through subtle pathways or meridians and 'centres' of energy, also know as chakras. One of the main ways that a skilful healer helps the body to heal is simply by stimulating and unblocking the meridians so our natural energies flow freely bringing mental, emotional and eventually physical balance and well being. This is the main way that most natural healing therapies work. Whether you use acupuncture, reflexology, Reiki, homeopathy or whatever they generally work to promote good health on a subtle energetic level first.

The physical therapies generally work to unblock and rebalance the energy system and the therapies that use remedies or healing 'energies', like homeopathy and Bach Flower Remedies, generally work to raise the quality of the internal energies so that blockages and imbalances naturally melt away. Some therapies like Reiki, crystal healing and shiatsu can be used to both unblock specific areas and raise the overall quality of life force energy. Also any 'good' healer whatever therapy they practice naturally transmits pure healing life force energy to their patients, many doctors even do this without realising! Just having a strong mental intention to help someone creates a kind of energetic pathway for life force energy to flow from one person to another. If this is accompanied by a sense of deep love or compassion very powerful healing can take place; at least the patient will feel better mentally and is more likely to view their situation from a more positive perspective.

The nervous system is the link between the subtle energetic body and the physical body. Some physical therapies, like massage, that do not directly work on the energy pathways or meridians work on them indirectly through the nervous system. However our body, nervous system, mind and internal energies are so intimately connected that a particular therapy may work on several of these areas at the same time to bring balance and healing to the whole. Even the therapies that work only on the mind like counselling and psychotherapy can have a positive influence on the physical body through this chain of close connections.

From a more general perspective we could say that Life Force Energy is the subtle foundation of all life, a sort of 'cosmic soup' that supports, nourishes and sustains the cycle of birth, life and death of all forms of life. Physical matter is made up of differing frequencies of energy. Solid objects are made up of energy vibrating at a very low or slow frequency. Less solid objects like water, air and subtle life force energy are vibrating incredibly fast. Buddhism, Chinese Medicine, Vedic Science and other similar eastern philosophies understand the concept of energy much better than we do. The basic principles of chinese medicine are explained in Appendix 4. This knowledge is also incorporated in to their religions in a way that explains the mystical and spiritual experiences that many devoted practitioners have. In these societies science, religion and art are not separated but seen simply as branches of the same tree of life.

One aspect of the Eastern understanding of God is as a Universal Life Force Energy, the source of all life. The life force in plants, trees, animals, humans, planets, stars and universes comes from this one source. It is this source of life, within our self, that we need to make contact with if we want to maintain or recreate good physical, mental and spiritual health. When we are in touch with this energy through prayer, meditation, taking a walk in the countryside or receiving healing we feel less 'separate' and increasingly 'whole' within ourselves and within the 'whole' of creation. We experience a sense of unity, we become more aware of our place or role in the great scheme of things and at the same time we feel support- ed, safe, open and confident in our ability to be all that we are. We can say that these spiritual or personal experiences are the 'essence' of healing. Without some significant inner movement towards wholeness any physical healing is just temporary. The real meaning of natural healing is to restore a person to wholeness and having a healthy body is only a small part of this. A 'good' natural healing treatment has the effect of restoring openness to our energy system so we can receive a well balanced flow of Universal Life Force Energy that is often cut off or restricted by illness. Being cut off from this life force is often the cause of much illness.

The subtle internal energies, or subtle winds as they are sometimes called in Buddhism, govern our mental as well as our physical health. The term subtle wind is very useful as it gives us a feel for what inner energy is and indicates that it is a light or gentle force that is moving or flowing.

There are two main types of Life Force Energy; Internal and External. As mentioned subtle internal life force energy is the energy that makes up our subtle body. Subtle external life force energy is the force or energy that makes plants and trees grow and exists within water, rocks, minerals, crystals and other natural objects. This energy is often harnessed for healing purposes as in the Bach Flower Remedies, Crystal Healing, Flower Essences and some Herbal Remedies. Even just a walk in the countryside or by the sea can have a calming and healing effect on us, there is so much pure external life force energy available in these places that it 'lifts' our own internal energies and this has a corresponding effect on our body and mind. If we spend too much time in built up areas or stressful environments where natural energies are restricted this may adversely affect our health, if we are unable to transform or 'rise above' these situations.

The most obvious or gross level of external life force energy is the movement we feel in the air on a windy day. Each of the four elements of fire, earth, wind and water has a life force energy. These different types of energy also exist within our body in their more subtle aspect and each has its own particular bodily functions to govern. For example the inner energy related to the wind element controls our digestion and is centred around the navel area, the inner energy related to the fire element is centred around the throat and controls our speech and the function of swallowing. When we are healthy these inner energies are well balanced and work together like a well trained team that cause our body to function correctly. If one energy is particularly weak or too strong this can cause health problems.

We can start to develop some awareness of our own energy system just by trying to remain conscious of how we physically and mentally feel in different situations and environments. It is easy to feel tired and run down in stressful environments and easy to feel uplifted and alive after a walk in a park or after eating food that is still 'alive' with energy. The more we 'notice' these simple experiences the more we will notice how they affect our inner energies and the corresponding relationship with our body and mind. We will also become increasingly aware of how other people affect our thoughts and feelings in a positive or negative way with their own energy.

Many people nowadays are becoming increasingly convinced in the power of 'living foods' for healing the body. This is raw food that still possesses life force energy as opposed to much of today's convenience food which is 'dead'. Also there is great interest in the more gentle exercise routines like yoga and Tai Chi which can greatly strengthen our inner energy system and promote good health. Again being aware of how our body and mind react to different types of food or exercise is very helpful. Developing this inner awareness will help us to know what to avoid and what to seek out if we want to keep good inner balance which can improve and maintain good health. Obviously we don't want this increased awareness to make us more selfish or over sensitive in an unhealthy way; if we avoid all difficult situations we will never become a stronger person and we will miss many opportunities to help others. So again developing inner balance needs to be accompanied by good judgement and a practical approach to life.

If we are treating others with healing therapies it is helpful to investigate why the patient became distant from their natural relationship with the Universal Life Force and how they can work to maintain a healthy relationship with it in the future. For some this may involve a personal spiritual revolution by rediscovering their own or a new religion or perhaps looking in to such practices as meditation, yoga, tai chi, counselling etc. But we do not have to be 'religious' to develop this special inner relationship with life. We cannot say that babies are religious but they definitely carry a special pure energy that comes from somewhere special! It is interesting to note that many well-known and respected spiritual teachers, healers and saints carry a similar energy. A light, playful and pure mind can put us back in the 'right place' and is also essential for good health to flourish.

Subtle internal and subtle external life force energy can be very similar energies. Sometimes the only difference is that internal life force energy has consciousness or 'mind' and cannot exist separately from it. Due to the close relationship between consciousness and internal life force energy it is easy to believe that the sense of closeness or companionship we feel towards trees, crystals, the Earth or other sources of external life force energy is because they possess a personal character or mind. Sensitive people can feel the energy within trees and because it feels similar to our own inner energy, which is intimate with our own mind, it feels as if the tree has a mind or character. External Life Force Energy, like that within trees, does not possess consciousness or mind, where as humans, animals, spirits and other beings possess consciousness and inner life force energies. However this does not make trees or plants any less special or sacred 'living' objects, if they are alive they possess life force energy, the breath of life, which can be harnessed in healing remedies to promote good health.

So our internal energies and our mind are inseparable, they exist almost as one and have a very intimate dependent relationship. In fact although we do not generally notice it our thoughts and feelings 'ride' on our internal energies. If we carry positive Internal Life Force Energy of a good quality, it is easier for us to develop positive states of mind and we generally attract positive life experiences and deal with problems more easily. If we consciously try to develop positive states of mind, like confidence, kindness and wisdom, this will raise the quality of our internal energies and in-turn improve our health and many other aspects of our lives. What we are doing with natural therapies is simply encouraging this process and creating the inner peace, space and other conditions conducive to the natural healing process. Often the success of the physical natural therapies like massage is simply due to the deep physical and mental relaxation created, when we are relaxed it is much easier for our inner energies to recharge and rebalance. In this way we can see the relationship between our physical health, our nervous system, our inner energies and our mind.

There are many conditions required for good health like good diet, regular light exercise, social and environmental circumstances, mental attitude etc. However there are times when good health is not so easily restored or maintained even when all the obvious conditions are present. Then we need to look for the deeper causes and solutions which will be examined later. However generally speaking we can see that with a good motivation natural therapies and remedies can greatly assist us in improving our own and others' quality of life. They help us become more whole and healthy beings on all levels and this in turn naturally benefits those around us and the friends and relatives of those we treat. When we help one person we are indirectly helping all those that our patient has a relationship with.

We need to encourage the people we treat to keep a happy mind, whatever their level of health as this is one of the major conditions required for good health. Our mind is one of the few things we can control in life if we learn how. We have a certain amount of control over our health but ultimately we will all become sick and have to face the process of dying and leaving behind all that we love and have worked for. If we can gradually learn throughout our life to keep a peaceful and happy mind and to be content and patient when things go wrong we will be a good role model for others and we will leave this world with a strong and healthy mind which can only lead to good things in the future. We will look at this approach to life in more detail in the next chapter.

The main part of this book explains the essential techniques for all the natural healing therapies that can easily be learnt from a book. Take your time to read through the chapters that really interest you, make plenty of notes and practice as much as you can and you will develop some very special healing skills. They all work well together and in their own right, you can do no harm with them and there are no serious side effects.

The main thing to avoid is putting to much pressure on yourself or others to get well; with natural healing techniques more is not always best. We have to accept that healing takes time and try to relax in to the natural healing process without expecting too much too soon. If you combine too many therapies and treat the patient too often they will feel worse so it is best to use only one or two of the following therapies once each week if you are giving a full treatment; aromatherapy, crystal healing, Reiki and reflexology. However short treatments for relaxation and gentle healing can be used every day. Techniques like meditation and yoga can be used every day along with herbal remedies and Bach Flower remedies. For homeopathy just follow the instructions that come with the remedies but it is probably best not to use the Bach Flower Remedies at the same time as they work in a similar way and it might be difficult to see which is working best.

Combining a few therapies can be much more effective than using just one or too many and in time you will become more attuned to your patients and instinctively feel what might be the best combination for different people. For example you can give someone reflexology and Reiki once a week, give them some advice on which herbal remedies to buy, check that they have a healthy diet and teach them some simple meditation techniques and advise them to take a little exercise like walking or swimming. Basically you can develop a healing plan together, this is very encouraging for the patient as they feel they are entering a structured and manageable programme which is taking them in a positive direction.

Try to help the patient to see that illness can be an opportunity for inner development. As well as putting effort in to getting well we should also try to relax and accept the limitations that illness imposes. If we cannot change something we should just try to relax and accept it. This attitude is not defeatist but shows that we have some wisdom. Illness or any difficulty in life is only a problem if it makes us unhappy. We can overcome our illness by accepting it and not allowing it to affect our inner peace. Our body might be affected by serious illness yet our mind can remain calm and peaceful.

In fact illness can be a cause of great inner development because it forces us to change and grow on the inside. Most human beings try to achieve happiness in the external world by accumulating wealth, possessions, friends etc. Of course these things bring us some happiness and feelings of security but this happiness is quite shallow and fragile and very dependant on the changing fortunes of life. But the happiness that we experience by becoming a better person is a very stable, deep and reliable form of happiness. Eventually if we pursue this way of life our mind will become so strong and peaceful that we will never feel unhappy, we become liberated from any kind of suffering because our mind is free. Attaining this level of inner development, known as nirvana or liberation in Buddhism, is the real meaning of healing because it meets our deepest need, the need to be happy for ever. All living beings have this wish and we all strive to fulfil it everyday. Whatever choices or decisions we make in life we do in order to increase our happiness or to decrease our unhappiness. Yet we will never fulfil this deep wish by continuing to be external beings, at some point we have to begin our own inner journey to lasting happiness. Happiness or fulfilment is just a state of mind - it comes from within so it is impossible to find the lasting peace of mind we long for in the external world. In this way illness can be a real blessing in disguise because it can help to start us on that inner journey towards wholeness and ultimate healing. If we want to be a genuine healer we have to think deeply about this over and over until we start to feel the truth of it, then we can gently communicate this to others in conversation or just by being a living example of someone bound for ultimate healing.

2
HEALING FROM WITHIN

We all know that a loving touch can heal, when we were children and we hurt ourselves perhaps the first person we ran to was our mother or whoever we felt loved us the most. Just being in the presence of someone who loves us makes us feel better. So we can say that a healing touch comes from a loving mind and that love is a healing energy or state of mind. If we are in any doubt about this we only have to think about the opposite. If we deliberately hurt someone at that time there is a lack of love in our mind, if we always had love in our mind we would never cause harm to others and we would always be thinking about their welfare. If there is love in a family there is harmony, open communication and a feeling of mutual support and the individuals generally experience better physical and mental health than in families without love. There is such a difference between human beings that have been raised in a loving environment and those that have suffered abuse or poor parenting, often regardless of external wealth. It is not always the case but often love sets us up for life and the opposite kind of childhood can be the beginning of many physical and mental health problems.

So it is obvious that the state of mind of the healer can greatly influence the success of a treatment, in fact this is one of the most important aspects of the therapeutic process. If we want to become a good healer, apart from learning complex healing techniques, one thing we can do straight away is make a decision to gradually develop a caring attitude towards others. This attitude towards others and life itself naturally creates a positive energy within our own body and mind and is one of the main requirements to becoming a successful healer and of course a happy person! The more time and effort we put in to finding love for others from within our self the more whole we will become. One of the amazing side effects of a stable feeling of love towards others is that it is very self healing. Many people believe that we need to love our self first before we can truly love others. This may be the right path for some, however by developing a mind of love towards others we naturally feel good inside. If we feel that we are working for the happiness of others, that we are playing our part in developing a better world, this gives us a great sense of fulfilment, confidence and self respect. In time this way of life can simply melt away many of our issues and hang ups that come from a difficult childhood or self preoccupation. Unpleasant states of mind like loneliness, lack of confidence, boredom, anger and so forth come from a strong sense of our own importance and a weak sense of the importance of others.

If we think about this carefully we will come to see clearly that when these heavy minds have a hold on us it is because at that time we are very focussed on our own wants and needs. Our world has become very small and all our mental and emotional energy and attention is inwardly focussed, which serves to feed and magnify our problems. At those times we have a strong sense of 'I' and a very weak sense of 'others'. Developing and expanding our sense of others steadily over time causes our sense of I or self importance to gradually fade and our quality of life becomes better and better. Becoming a better person in this way makes us a much better healer. When our mind is wide, expansive and relaxed with love, we naturally feel interested in others and helping to make our world a better place. Consequently the quality of the inner energy we carry is much higher. Compassion is very healing and there are many accounts of deeply compassionate people like Jesus and Buddha and modern healers like Dr Edward Bach who were sometimes able to heal simply through the power of touch. Their own inner energies have become so pure through developing deep compassion that they are able to naturally transmit this inner healing energy to others.

Generally we are brought up to feel that our own happiness is more important than the happiness of others and we instinctively feel that to fulfil our deep wish to be happy we must pursue the things that we feel will make us happy. In reality this is a completely deceptive view because ultimate happiness can only be achieved by letting go of our own selfish desires. Ironically it is our own sense of self importance that is the cause of all our unhappiness. Striving for our own happiness actually takes us further away from it! This is a tough idea to accept as ultimately it means we have to mentally let go of everything that currently makes us feel secure and happy and of course our deep sense of I finds this an appalling prospect. But if we adopt this inner way of life gently and progress at our own pace we will only find more and more natural joy and happiness arising from within as we let go of the artificial happiness that comes from external sources. This raises lots of questions like, do I have to let go of relationships and my car and my favourite foods? We do but only in our mind, we don't have to change anything externally. Actually our relationships only become better, when our need for others becomes less our love for them becomes pure and less conditional. We feel happier because of this and others feel happier because they are getting more love. We will even find that the enjoyment we derive from food or clothes or entertainment is of a higher quality again because we are not so dependent on these things, the need or attachment is gone and there is more space in our mind. This way of life is a real protection against the changing fortunes of life, if good things come our way that's great but when things don't work out the way we planned it is easier for us to accept because we didn't have a deep need for a particular outcome. One way to gradually adopt this new way of thinking is to simply remember a simple phrase like 'happiness from within'. Spend a few minutes at the start of each day just thinking or meditating on it and try to remember your good feelings or intentions throughout the day. When you are faced with an opportunity to indulge your desires you don't necessarily have to deny yourself, especially to begin with, as this will just make you too unhappy. Just gently remind yourself that lasting happiness can only come from within, happiness from external sources is only short lived and deceptive. If we are sensible like this in time our desire for external happiness will lessen its grip on our mind and we will start to feel some real inner freedom and natural happiness. Because our mind is simply a creature of habit if you persevere for a long time you will definitely adopt this special way of life on a deeper level, it will become second nature.

Many might disagree with the idea of putting others first and give examples of business people or athletes who have strived for self motivated achievements and found happiness in success. If such people have done this for their own selfish gain the sense of happiness is really quite shallow, we have all met people who have been successful and need to tell everyone in order to feel good inside, obviously such people are not deeply happy. However if they have been motivated by the wish to be a good example and to encourage others to better themselves then the sense of achievement is much deeper and more genuine. Another reason 'successful' people feel a sense of achievement is that they have challenged their sense of I and beaten it. People who lack confidence and make an effort to overcome their fears feel a great sense of freedom and achievement. Lots of successful business people, entertainers or adventures fall in to this category and although it appears that pursuing their own happiness has worked in fact it is the destruction of their own negative sense of I that makes them feel good. Indirectly these people do much good for the world because they inspire us all to set our sights a little higher and overcome our own inner barriers to happiness. Often such people naturally develop the desire to share what they have learnt with others because they have found a path away from the unhappiness or inner limitations they experienced earlier in life. They are encouraging others to work towards a more positive sense of I.

Taking this line of thought to a more spiritual level we can say that the most positive sense of I is no I! Through following correct spiritual teachings we can become so focussed on the welfare of others that we loose our sense of I. We don't need a strong sense of I in order to be happy, in fact it just gets in the way and causes all kinds of problems! For example we all have very strong desires and wishes, we all want a good house, car, partner, friends etc. The stronger our sense of I or self importance the stronger our level of desire and the stronger our sense of disappointment when our desires are not met. Our strong sense of I is like an inner blockage that prevents an experience of natural happiness arising naturally from within. If we didn't have a strong sense of I we would be naturally relaxed, happy and content. It takes time and hard work to develop inner happiness and because our strong sense of I wants happiness now it keeps forcing us to forget about the inner path and keeps us trying to find happiness in the external world. It is like having a spoilt child inside that does not want to listen to good sense!

Directly or indirectly all the religions of the world teach that happiness comes from reducing our sense of self importance either through learning to sincerely care for others or by letting go to the will of a much greater and wiser power than our own sense of self. If you want to know more about the Buddhist path see appendix 1.

We need to discover a direct inner feeling for these ideas for our self in our own time. It is important that we try to do this because we need to share these ideas with others if we want to help them achieve good health on all levels. Everyone will be open to this way of living if we communicate it skilfully because everyone knows that love is a beneficial state of mind and that to feel love and happiness from within is very healing. People also understand that strong selfish states of mind like anger are not pleasant to experience and can lead to stress and illness.

When we are ill much of our suffering comes from our own mind. This is why some people are able to bear discomfort and pain much more easily than others, they simply don't notice it as much. Our mind has the ability to exaggerate or ignore discomfort. We probably know people who habitually turn the slightest problem in to a drama and find it easy to become stressed, over excited or depressed! We probably also know others who are able to simply accept whatever problems come their way with a relaxed and positive attitude. The difference between these two types of people is just the mind or more specifically their habits of mind. Our character or personality is not set in stone we can change the habits of a lifetime if we just put our mind to it and try to approach life from a different perspective. Of course this takes time; anything worth doing requires time, effort and commitment. But this journey of transforming our mind is well worth the effort. If illness is the cause of our beginning this special journey how can we say that illness is a problem?

Again this is very helpful advice to share with others because even if our body is suffering an illness which is beyond our control we can always do something with our mind. There is no reason why people who are ill should not live a full and inspiring life. Obviously they may experience severe physical limitations but the mind is only bound by the physical world if we allow it to be. In reality the mind has no boundaries; it has incredible power and potential completely beyond the understanding of most healthy people! Because we have become such 'external' beings we never even glimpse our inner potential, yet realising our inner potential, not external development, is the real meaning of human life, not external development.

If we are mainly interested in healing our self then it can be really helpful to pursue some kind of spiritual path or personal growth strategy like counselling or therapy alongside using natural healing therapies. Perhaps we need to rediscover our own religion or start to look elsewhere. Healing our mind and finding some inner peace and harmony from within can really support the physical healing process. We need to look within and try to understand who we are, how we became that way and how we can build a better quality of life through spiritual or personal growth. Again if we are trying to help others we can encourage them to do the same. Obviously we do not want to impose our own views or religion on them but rather try to listen and very gently encourage them to identify what it is within that needs to change or develop. Together you need to explore the options that might facilitate such inner work. Don't push, try to allow it to happen naturally, if you feel drawn to suggesting something that instinctively feels right then go ahead, it might be just right or at least sow a seed for later contemplation.

Physical healing without some kind of inner healing is almost a waste of time. We all derive much happiness from being physically healthy, in fact for most people a huge part of their quality of life is related to having good health. If you are not sure of the truth of this just imagine how you would feel if you developed a difficult illness like multiple sclerosis or cancer. You would probably feel deeply distressed and this shows that we are very external beings; we need so many external conditions, relationships and possessions in order to be happy. Yet these things are so unreliable! Even if we have many years of good health, life passes very quickly and our health eventually begins to degenerate and when our life comes to an end we have to let go of everything. At that time if we have not built up some inner happiness the process of death will be very difficult. Our human life is an opportunity to understand this truth, to become more whole and healthy beings from within and live life in an enlightened way. Again if we can understand this and keep it in our heart we will become a much more effective healer on every level as well as a very happy and fulfilled human being.

3
AROMATHERAPY

Aromatherapy is the combination of therapeutic massage and essential oils. Like many complementary therapies aromatherapy has its roots deep in the history of mankind. We all know that a loving touch can help to relax and heal the mind and the body. When we feel depressed or anxious the first thing we often seek is some physical contact, the earliest human beings must have been just the same. Feeling loved and experiencing this through touch can be an important part of a healthy life.

We also know that our ancestors used herbs and plants for healing and must have built up an intimate knowledge of their individual characteristics. It cannot have taken long for them to combine basic massage with some form of herbal mixture in order to try to heal the body.

Aromatherapy, in its modern format, began with the Egyptians, who used the method of infusion to extract the oils from aromatic plants which were used for medicinal and cosmetic purposes as well as embalming. Ancient Egyptians used substance and scents of specific plants for religious rituals, as certain smells could help raise consciousness or promote a state of tranquillity. Frankincense was burned at dawn as an offering to the sun and myrrh was offered to the moon. The Egyptians understood the principles of aromatherapy and incorporated it into their cooking as well. Specific herbs helped the digestive process, protected against infection, or built the immune system.

Ayurveda, the traditional and ancient medical system of India, uses dried and fresh herbs, as well as aromatic massage, as important aspects of healing. The Greeks acquired most of their medical knowledge from the Egyptians and used it to further their own discoveries. They found that the fragrance of some flowers was stimulating while others had relaxing properties. They also used olive oil as the base oil which absorbed the aroma from the herbs or flowers and this was then used for both cosmetic and medicinal purposes.

Hypocrites, the 'Father of Medicine', was the first to study the effects of essential oils. He believed that a daily aromatic bath and scented massage would promote good health. For at least 1200 years a book about herbal medicine written by another Greek physician named Pedacius Dioscorides was the Western world's standard medical reference and many of the remedies he mentions are still in used in Aromatherapy today.

Essential oils have an immediate impact on our sense of smell. When essential oils are inhaled, olfactory receptor cells are stimulated and the impulse is transmitted to the emotional centre of the brain, or limbic system. The limbic system is connected to areas of the brain linked to memory, breathing, and blood circulation, as well as the endocrine glands which regulate hormone levels in the body. The properties of the oil, the fragrance and its effects, stimulate and balance these systems. When used in massage, essential oils are not only inhaled, but absorbed through the skin as well. They penetrate the tissues and find their way into the bloodstream where they are transported to the organs and various systems of the body.

Essential oils can be used either alone or in combinations to create a desired effect. The oils are found in different parts of the plant such as the flowers, twigs, leaves and bark, or in the rind of fruit. For example, in roses it is found in the flowers, in basil it is in the leaves, in sandalwood in the wood, and so on. The methods used to extract the oil are time consuming and expensive and require a high degree of expertise. Due to the large quantity of plant material required pure essential oils are expensive but they are also highly effective, only a few drops at a time are required to achieve the desired effect. Synthetic oils are available at a lesser price, but they do not have the healing power of the natural oils.

Essential oils are often described by their 'note'. The three categories of classification are top note, middle note and base note, and these terms relate to the rate at which they evaporate or how long the fragrance will last. Top notes are the most stimulating and uplifting oils. They are strongly scented, but the perfume lasts only for approximately 3 - 24 hours. Middle notes are the next longest lasting, at about 2 - 3 days, the perfume is less potent than that of top note oils. Base notes are the slowest oils to evaporate, lasting up to one week. They have a sweet, soothing scent and a relaxing, comforting effect on the body.

The use of essential oils in massage is a fantastic way to maximize the healing power of the massage itself. When combined with essential oils, a massage can have a powerful calming or energizing effect, depending on the oil chosen and the strokes of the masseur, quick movements will stimulate and slow movements relax. When using essential oils in massage, always dilute the oils in a 'carrier' oil prior to application to the skin. Essential oils are very powerful concentrates, and unless indicated otherwise, should not be directly applied to the skin or irritation can result.

Carrier oils hold the essential oil, there are a wide variety available including the following:

Almond Oil - very easily absorbed by the skin, very smooth, has little smell, keeps well, contains vitamin D and has beneficial effects on hair, dry skin and brittle nails

Apricot Kernel Oil - light, contains Vitamin A, particularly good for use on the face if the skin is dry or aging

Avocado Oil - heavy, rich in nutrients, very good for dry, aging and sensitive skins

Evening Primrose Oil - helpful for skin conditions such as eczema and psoriasis, only keeps for about 2 months after opening

Grapeseed Oil - light, good for oily skin, one of the least expensive oils

Hazelnut Oil - penetrates the skin very easily and is deeply nourishing

Jojoba Oil - light, rich in vitamin E, beneficial for spots, acne, dandruff and dry scalp

Olive Oil - can be used, but has a strong smell which may compete with the essential oil

Peach Kernel Oil - light, contains vitamins A & E, very good for the face

Soya Oil - easily absorbed, rich in vitamin E

Sunflower Oil - contains essential fatty acids, rich in vitamin E, has a slightly nutty smell

Wheat germ Oil - contains vitamins A, B, C and E, firms and tones the skin, reduces blemishes, can help to reduce scar tissue and stretch marks, has a strong smell

When combining oils to be used in massage have the proper supplies to hand. You will need dark bottles (for protection from the light), the 2oz size works very well and can be obtained easily. Using a small funnel fill the container half full until you have about 1oz of carrier oil. Add 12-15 drops of essential oil, place the lid on the container and shake well. You can combine up to three essential oils of your choice to comprise the 12-15 drops. Make small quantities as outlined above or you may end up with too much, blended oils can turn rancid fairly quickly. Store them in a cool dark place with the lid tightly closed and they will last up to three months.

There is a variety of ways to fill your surroundings with the pleasant aromas of essential oils. They can be added to humidifiers, vaporisers, the molten wax of a candle, the dish of a diffuser mixed with water, water in a bath or even combined with water in a spray bottle. Simply add a few drops of your favourite oil.

A FULL TREATMENT

This section will provide you with all the techniques and knowledge required to give a full aromatherapy treatment. In the following section there is a list of essential oils and their appropriate uses. Anyone can give a really effective treatment, it just takes plenty of practice and patience. A full treatment can be quite tiring so at the start don't do too many in one day. Quality is much better than quantity, so take your time, learn each step of the massage systematically and you will become a very accomplished aromatherapist.

The sequence of techniques given here is just suggested, but also tried and tested. You can change the order or add new techniques that you discover or that others teach you. Also you need to be in touch with your patient's needs and wishes and avoid any techniques that they do not find beneficial. Of course you need to make sure that your techniques never harm so check whether you patient has any medical conditions that need to be taken in to consideration. The most obvious is a back problem or joint/muscle problems. A heavy/vigorous massage can damage sensitive parts of the body so if you are aware of some weakness it is always better to be too light than too firm, you can always increase the pressure in future treatments if there is no adverse reaction. Also remember that a vigorous massage might feel wonderful at the time but the aggravation of any weakness in the body can be delayed, so again be gentle if you are unsure.

Two of the most important factors in a successful massage are that both you and your patient need to be very comfortable. You can use a therapy couch to give a massage or the patient can lay on the floor on a soft mat or duvet or sometimes a soft carpet covered with a few towels will suffice. The room needs to be warm and soft music and incense or an aroma burner are a wonderful addition.

The patient needs to feel completely relaxed to gain the most from the treatment and this might not happen the first time so don't worry. Also they might not be happy to be undressed so you can always offer to massage through a T-shirt and light trousers, but obviously without oils. Unless you are very close to the patient it is always better to allow them to undress whilst you are out of the room, show them how to cover themselves with a large towel and tell them where to lay down. It is very useful to practice all this on people you know and get their feedback before you begin treating others.

Warm hands are essential, you can massage your own hands and/or place them in warm water for a while to raise their temperature. Unless it is the first treatment you should have prepared a massage oil as explained earlier then simply put a small amount in one hand, spread it evenly over two hands and begin the massage. If you use too much your hands will slip uncontrollably, too little will cause your hands to stick rather than glide smoothly, you will find out through experience what is just right.

You can also warm your carrier oil by standing the bottle in a bowl of warm water for a few minutes before the massage.

Generally try to keep your back fairly straight during the massage; this will reduce the possibility of back ache. Initially your stomach and lower back muscles will ache after each massage but in time they will become stronger and your back will not suffer. If you are using a therapy couch this will cause less stress on your back. If your patient is laid on the floor do not sit astride them, as this can feel too overpowering. You should be able to perform the whole massage by simply moving around the body. Make sure you are not wearing jewellery and that you finger nails are short, wear clothes that are comfortable and allow you to move freely. Wash your hands between treatments and drink a glass of water to keep hydrated. The patient may need a drink when they are finished and some tissues and a comfortable chair can always be useful if the patient feels a little emotional as sometimes happens during any healing therapy.

It is always good to ask for feedback after the treatment and this also gives the patient the opportunity to talk about anything that might be on their mind. Also, before a treatment, don't be afraid to ask the patient what kind of massage they would like and what they would like to get out of this kind of therapy. You will need time like this to get to know your patient well.

A full treatment comprises the following seven sections:
1 Back and Shoulders
2 Arms
3 Legs
4 Knees, Ankles and Feet
5 Abdomen

6 Chest, Neck and Shoulders

7 Face

You do not always have to do a full body massage, if you only have 10-20 minutes you could just do a back massage or neck and shoulders. To begin your patient should be in a comfortable position lying face down; they may find it more comfortable to have a pillow or just a towel rolled up for their head to rest on. It is possible to create a face support by rolling up a large towel and forming a circle shape so that the patient's face can be supported although it is important that breathing is completely unrestricted. The patient should know that they can move if they become uncomfortable at any point during the treatment.

To begin, pull the towel down to just above the buttocks and place your palms on the patient's back at the level of the heart and try to feel a 'connection'. You can say a silent prayer or set a positive affirmation like 'may this person receive the maximum benefit from this treatment' or 'may this massage be a powerful healing action for body and mind'.

If you are sensitive this brief quiet time will enable you to feel what kind of massage your patient requires, it will enable you to feel if your patient's energies are weak or strong and what emotional or mental problems the patient may have. If you do not feel anything don't worry, just use this time to develop a peaceful mind and a positive intention.

1 BACK AND SHOULDER MASSAGE

Effleurage – Beginning at the base of the spine, fingers pointing towards the head, lightly press down and then push your hands all the way to the top of the shoulders. Continue the motion along either side of the shoulders and then back down the sides of the back to where you started, as shown in the diagram. Continue this motion for a few minutes so that you have covered the whole back several times. Again don't press down too hard especially on the first treatment until you know what your patient needs and enjoys. Also avoid the buttock area unless you have a close relationship with your patient. With all these techniques you need to maintain a smooth and continuous movement, not breaking contact with the body unless necessary.

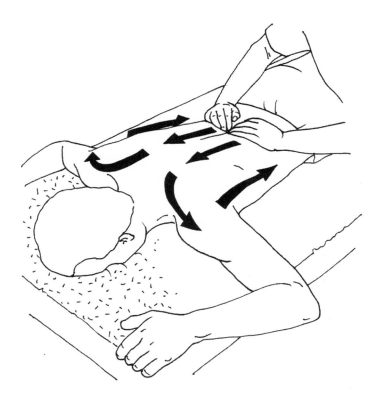

Kneading – This is a little more deep and energetic but still gentle. Again beginning at the base of the back use your thumbs and fingers to create a rhythmic kneading action moving from the spine to the side of the body which is further away from you. Repeat this all the way up to the shoulders and all over the shoulders and the base of the neck. Then move round to the other side of your patient and repeat this action.

This can be a very deep form of massage technique so again be gentle to begin with especially around the shoulders and neck where people tend to carry much tension. If you apply too much pressure to an area of tension this can sometimes even make it worse! Your patient knows what feels good so don't be afraid to check with them if they feel OK. You can repeat this technique several times until you think it has served its purpose.

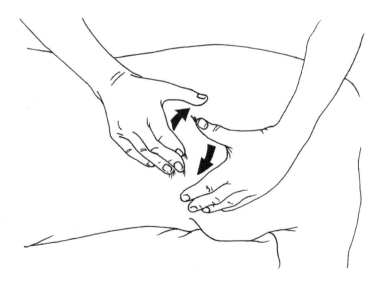

Thumb Circles – This next technique is for releasing tension in the muscles that support the spine. Use your thumbs to create small circular movements one after another in the same area. Do not work on the spine

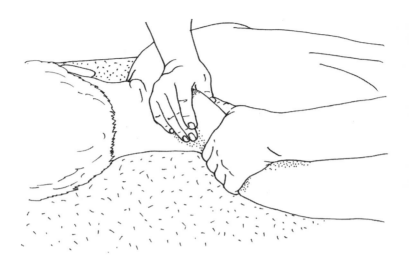

itself; keep your movements only on the muscles on either side of the spine. Begin at the base of the spine and work your way all the way up one side until you reach the base of the neck, then do the other side again from the base first. You can do this two or three times for each side. Many people carry knots of tension in these areas around the spine which result from mental/emotional stress and sometimes poor posture or excessive manual work. These knots of tension can be quite sensitive so again a light touch might be best to begin with. An alternative way is to use the tips of the fingers of one hand supported by the other hand, as shown in the diagram on page 42, and massage one side of the spine and then the other.

Thumb Press – Again beginning at the base of the spine, position the tips of your thumbs either side of the spine in the centre of the muscles that you have just massaged with the previous technique. Press gently and hold for a few seconds, then release and move your thumbs toward the head but only about 3-5cm then press and hold again, repeat this all the way to the base of the neck without touching the spine. In the areas where there is a knot of tension you can hold for longer. Keep checking that the patient is relaxed and comfortable with what you are doing.

Stroking – Stand to one side of the patient, again beginning at the base of the back place your hands side by side palms down and fingers and thumbs together, begin a smooth pulling and pushing motion, as you push one hand away from you draw the other towards you. Slowly work your way up the back and repeat 2 or 3 times. Like most massage techniques it can be performed in a relaxing or invigorating way depending on the

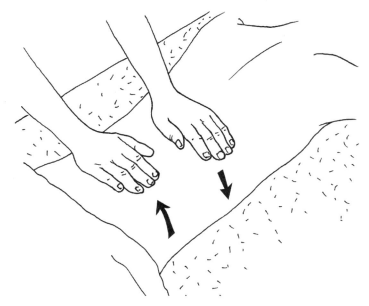

needs of your patient.

Stretching – Beginning in the centre of the back place your palms together so that the base of your hands are touching the back over the centre of the spine. Apply a little pressure and separate your hands so that one travels to the base of the spine and the other moves up to the neck, it should feel like you are stretching the skin and muscles. Then return to the starting point and repeat this motion but this time stretch diagonally in one direction and then in the other with the next stroke.

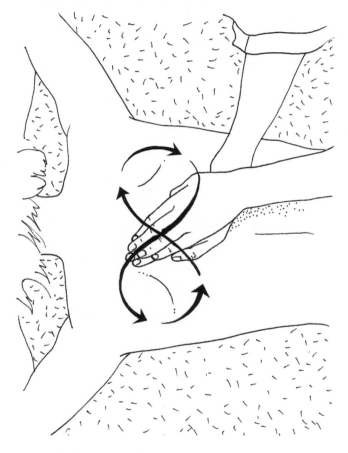

Figure of Eight – Again beginning at the base of the back use your hands with fingers and thumbs together to create a figure of eight pattern over the whole of the base of the back. Once you have done this a few times move up the back so that you eventually cover the whole area.

To complete the back massage you can do a light effleurage motion again as described earlier, then cover the patient's back with the towel. If you want to give your patient an invigorating massage there are three extra techniques you can use on the back; cupping, pummelling and hacking.

Cupping – Keep you fingers and thumbs together and form a shallow 'cup' with each hand. Starting at the base of the back use a quick slapping motion with alternate hands, this creates a slight vacuum as you cup the body. Don't use too much force, especially near the spine, but if you are too gentle it will not have the desired effect. Work your way in lines from the base to the top so the whole back is covered.

Pummelling – Form a fist with both hands and use a gentle 'bouncing' motion to pummel the back in lines from top to bottom and back, again avoid directly touching the spine.

Hacking – This is a similar action to pummelling but instead you hold your fingers and thumbs together to create a 'flat' hand and use the underside to stimulate the body. From top to bottom cover the whole back but avoid the vertebrae.

2 ARMS

Effleurage – Again you will need some oil spread evenly across both hands and begin with a gentle effleurage of the lower and upper arms. This means using the flat of your hands with the fingers and thumbs together to stroke the whole arm in both directions with one hand following the other, you can also cover part of the shoulder area to make sure you are covering the whole arm. Move from one side of the patient to the other as you treat the corresponding arm.

Kneading – This motion uses the fingers and thumb to hold and knead/massage the various muscles of the arm both front and back, use

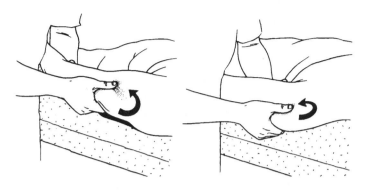

whichever hand feels most natural and use the other hand to support the arm.

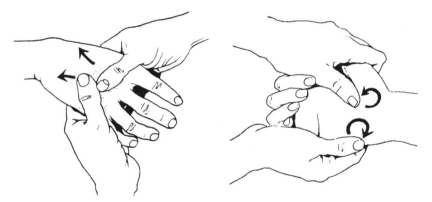

Thumb Technique – Massage the front and back of each hand and wrist using your thumbs to do the main work.

Finger Pull – Use a sliding and pulling motion on each finger from the base to the tip, be careful not to apply too much pressure especially if the joints are sensitive or stiff.

You can use all these techniques several times until the arm is completely relaxed. Remember you need to allow enough time to complete a full massage so do not spend too much time on any one technique unless there is a need or request from the patient.

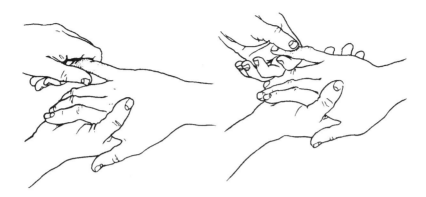

3 LEGS

Begin by massaging the back of the legs while the patient is still lying face down by using the effleurage and kneading techniques as shown below.

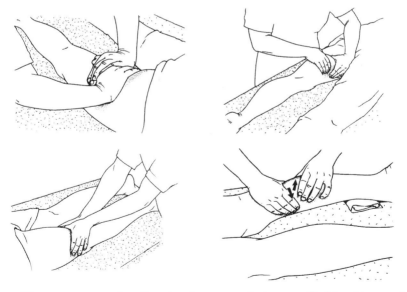

There are a couple of optional extra techniques called hacking and cupping (gentle slapping with a 'cupped hand') which you can use on the thigh and calf muscles as shown below.

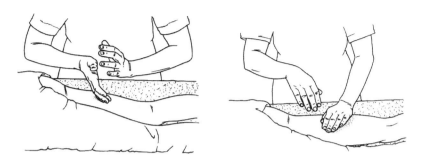

Ask your patient to turn over when they are ready, hold the towel whilst they do this so that it stays very close to the body and they remain fully covered. If you think they would feel more comfortable offer to leave the room while they turn over and recover themselves. Begin by moving the towel so that only one leg is exposed up to the top of the thigh. It is worth mentioning that a rolled up towel placed behind the knee at the start of the treatment can make the patient feel more comfortable especially if they have a back problem.

Effleurage – Again start with a gentle effleurage on the front and sides of the leg working from the top of the foot to the top of the thigh.

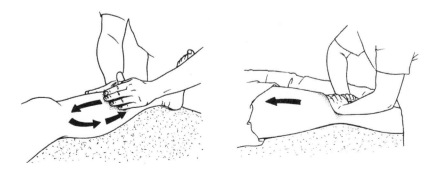

Kneading – Cover the whole of the front and sides of the leg, but do not apply too much pressure to the shin area, you can use your thumbs to knead this area as shown below.

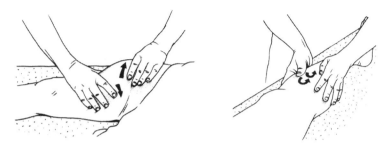

Then lift the leg by holding one hand under the knee and one on the ankle so that you can work the back of the leg. First kneed the calf, as shown below, and then the thigh and then gently replace the leg in its original position.

KNEES ANKLES AND FEET.

Knees – Use your palms with fingers and thumbs together to massage in a circular motion around the knee one way and then the other, you can also use your thumbs to massage around the knee cap. This can feel uncomfortable if too much pressure is used so keep a light touch.

Ankles – Again use your finger tips to massage all around each ankle.

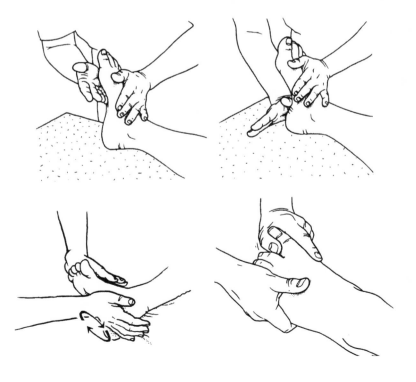

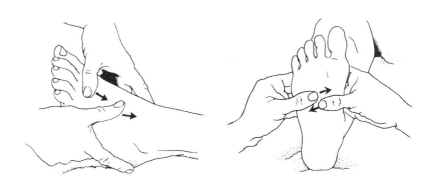

Feet – Start by stretching the foot, put one hand under the heel but do not lift the foot. Use the other to push the top of the foot away from you and then pull it towards you so that it is fully stretched in both directions. Keep both hands in the same position and rotate the foot one way and then the other so that the ankle is loosened. Then place both your hands either side of the widest part of the foot, just below the toes. Apply a little pressure and slowly twist the foot one way and then the other. Then use both hands to effleurage and knead as shown below, you can do the same with your thumbs if you want to apply more pressure.

As with all the massage techniques you can repeat each of them a few times until you feel they have done their job. Finally use your first two fingers and thumb of one hand to hold the base of each toe and gently rotate it one way and then the other. If you want to do more detailed reflexology at this point use the diagrams and techniques given in chapter 4, but make sure you don't do too much as this can put too much healing pressure on the body.

5 ABDOMEN

Once you have completed and covered the legs you can uncover the stomach area.

Effleurage - Begin with a gentle effleurage over the whole stomach area, be careful not to apply too much pressure. You can also use a circular motion as well as the normal inline massage technique that is used on the back, use whichever feels right or whichever the patient prefers.

You can also apply a gentle kneading and/or figure of eight technique as shown below.

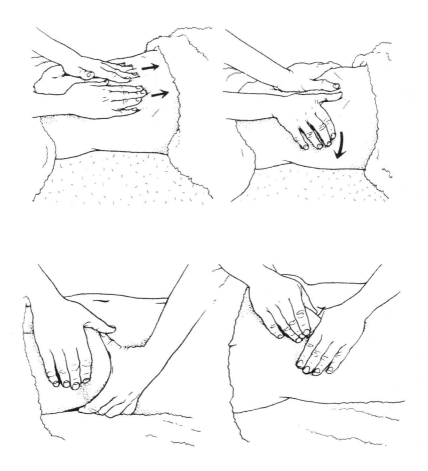

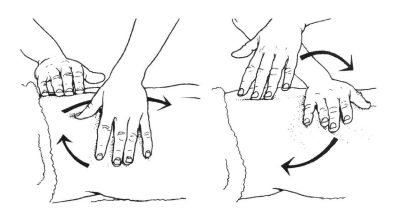

6 CHEST, NECK AND SHOULDERS

Once you have covered the stomach, position yourself behind the patient's head. With oil on your hands effleurage the upper chest area being careful to avoid the upper part of the breasts if you are treating a woman and to keep that area covered.

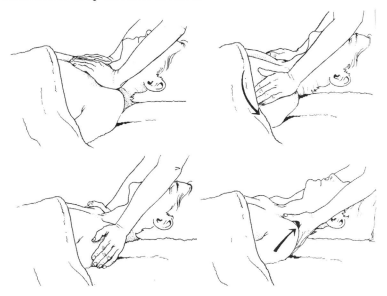

Finger Press – Beginning in the centre of the chest place each finger between the ribs, press gently and hold. Then move your fingers about 5cm apart and repeat until you reach the sides of the rib cage, again avoid applying pressure to any part of the breast. Alternatively you can use your thumbs and do one row at a time as shown below.

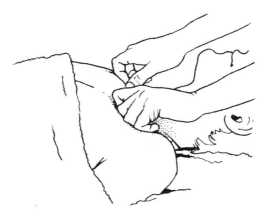

Shoulder Press – Place your palms on each shoulder, apply gentle pressure to one and then the other and then both together. Then use your thumbs to massage the front and tops of the shoulders a little more deeply as shown below.

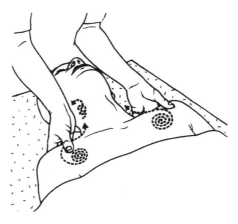

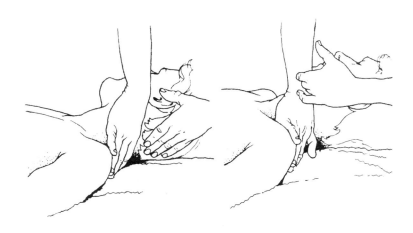

Neck Massage – Use your hands with fingers and thumbs together or just your finger tips to massage the sides and back of the neck. Small circular movements and strokes seem to be most effective. It is very important not to apply too much pressure especially on the sides of the neck where important arteries run, and only use a very light touch on the throat/front of the neck. You can apply a little more pressure around the back of the neck where people tend to carry tension.

7 FACE

Forehead – Stay in the same position behind the patient's head. Once you have covered the face with a light amount of oil (just use your fingers to do this with a light effleurage motion) begin the face massage by 'stretching' the forehead area. Place your palms together, fingers and thumbs touching, so that the under side of each hand is lightly touching the centre of the forehead, apply a little more pressure and open your hands so that they start to 'stretch' the skin and muscles. Stop when you get to the sides of the head and use your finger tips to gently massage the temples in a circular motion. When applying oil to the face it is very important to avoid any contact with the eyes, so again use a light amount of oil and be careful to avoid any drips that might splash the eye.

Eyebrows – use a gentle pinching motion, with thumb and first fingers, to massage the eye brows from one side to the other and then use a smoothing stroke in the direction that the hair grows. Again be careful to avoid the eyes.

Cheeks and Mouth – Use your finger tips to gently massage the cheeks using circular movements and then stretching movements going away from the nose to the side of the head. Continue this kind of massage around the mouth and along the jaw line. You can also spend some time massaging the ears between finger and thumbs.

Scalp – To finish you can use your fingers tips to massage the whole scalp area; this is stimulating as well as relaxing and is a good way to help the patient become more alert as the massage draws to a close.

Don't rush your patient to sit up, give them plenty of time and make sure they are fully awake before they leave, especially if they are going to drive home. A cup of tea and a biscuit can help people to wake up if they have been asleep or deeply relaxed.

This massage routine is a general guide for a complete massage. The techniques can be varied to suit your patient and as you become more familiar you will discover new ones of your own that may work better, so don't be afraid to experiment on a friend and see what feels good, if you are unsure always use a light pressure to begin with.

Also remember that two of the most important things are your state of mind and your motivation for giving a massage. If you are relaxed and looking forward to helping someone you will be a channel for positive healing energy and this energy will be magnified if your motivation is pure, that means without self interest. If you are giving a massage in order to impress or show off or if you want something in return this is a poor healing action and doesn't bring much good to the world. But if your wish is to help others in order to make the world a little better this creates a very pure and powerful healing action. It is our intention/motivation that makes our actions full of positive power or just self interest.

INDEX OF OILS AND THEIR USES

Use this section to get to know the healing properties of each essential oil. New oils are being discovered all the time but the following oils are those most commonly used for healing purposes. Don't buy them all at once! Just look through the list and decide which you are most likely to use on yourself, friends and family. If you start treating other people you can buy oils that might be useful for them after the first treatment when you have a better understanding of what they need.

IMPORTANT NOTE: Always look carefully at the 'caution'. This shows when the oil should not be used or only used in a very diluted form.

Basil

Effects: Uplifting and stimulating
Note: Top note
Aroma: Fresh, Sweet, Spicy
Combines with: Citrus oils, Frankincense, Geranium
Properties: Analgesic, Antidepressant, Antiseptic, Antispasmodic, Uplifting
Uses: Bronchitis, Colds, Constipation, Insect Bites, Mental Fatigue, Migraine, Nervous Tension, Rheumatism, Sinus Congestion
Caution: May cause irritation to sensitive skin. Use well diluted. Not to

be used during pregnancy.

Bergamot

Effects: Refreshing and uplifting

Note: Top note

Aroma: Sweet, Spicy

Combines with: Chamomile, Geranium, Lavender

Properties: Antidepressant, Antiseptic, Antispasmodic

Uses: Abscesses, Acne, Boils, Chicken Pox, Colds, Cold Sores, Cystitis, Flatulence, Loss of Appetite, Mouth Infections, Sore Throat

Caution: Bergamot is a photo sensitizer (increases the skins reaction to sunlight making it more likely to burn) so it should not be used when exposed to sunlight or tanning beds. Bergamot has antispasmodic properties and therefore should be avoided during pregnancy.

Black Pepper

Effects: Stimulating

Note: Middle note

Aroma: Warm, Peppery

Combines with: Lavender, Rosemary, Sandalwood

Properties: Diuretic, Expectorant, Stimulant

Uses: Chilblains, Colds, Constipation, Digestive Problems, Flatulence, Heartburn, Indigestion, Loss of Appetite, Muscle Aches and Pains, Sinus Congestion

Caution: Black Pepper may irritate sensitive skin. Use well diluted. Avoid use during pregnancy.

Chamomile

Effects: Soothing, Relaxing

Note: Middle note

Aroma: Sweet, Herbal, Fruity

Combines with: Bergamot, Geranium, Lavender

Properties: Analgesic, Antibacterial, Antiseptic, Digestive Stimulant

Uses: Acne, Blisters, Boils, Colitis, Depression, Digestive Problems, Flatulence, Gout, Headaches, Indigestion, Irritable Bowel Syndrome, Neuralgia, Nervous Tension (anxiety, fear), Rheumatism, Skin Conditions (dermatitis, eczema, psoriasis)

Caution: Chamomile may cause skin irritation. Not to be used in early pregnancy.

Cedarwood

Effects: Soothing, Strengthening

Note: Base note

Aroma: Woody

Combines with: Bergamot, Rosemary, Sandalwood

Properties: Antifungal, Antiseptic, Astringent, Expectorant, Sedative

Uses: Arthritis, Bronchitis, Cellulite, Cystitis, Dandruff (blend with Rosemary),

Skin Conditions (such as acne, eczema, oily skin)

Caution: Cedarwood may cause skin irritation to sensitive skin. Do not use during pregnancy.

Clary Sage

Effects: Warming

Note: Top/Middle note

Aroma: Sweet, Spicy, Herbal

Combines with: Geranium, Lavender, Rose

Properties: Anti-inflammatory, Antiseptic, Antispasmodic, Sedative

Uses: Asthma, Depression, Digestive Problems, Exhaustion, Muscle Cramps and Spasms, PMS Relief, Respiratory Problems

Caution: Do not use Clary Sage during pregnancy. Clary Sage is highly sedative so do not use before driving or other activities requiring a high level of focus and concentration.

Clove

Effects: Warming

Note: Base/Middle note

Aroma: Sweet, Spicy, Fresh

Combines with: Lavender, Orange, Ylang Ylang

Properties: Analgesic, Expectorant, Stimulant

Uses: Bronchitis, Colds, Indigestion, Infected Wounds, Insect Repellent, Mouth Sores, Muscle and Nerve Tension, Room Disinfectant, Toothache.

Caution: Clove is highly irritating to the skin and must be diluted to concentrations less than 1% prior to use.

Cypress

Effects: Relaxing, Refreshing

Note: Middle/Base note

Aroma: Sweet, Refreshing

Combines with: Citrus oils, Juniper, Lavender

Properties: Antispasmodic, Astringent, Diuretic, Expectorant

Uses: Asthma, Bronchitis, Cough, Oedema, Haemorrhoids, Menopause Symptoms, Menstrual Symptoms, Muscle and Nerve Tension, Oily Skin and/or Hair, Rheumatism

Caution: Cypress has antispasmodic properties and is therefore probably best avoided during pregnancy.

Eucalyptus

Effects: Balancing, Stimulating

Note: Top/Middle note

Aroma: Camphor, Woody

Combines with: Juniper, Lavender, Marjoram

Properties: Analgesic, Anti-inflammatory, Antiseptic, Antiviral, Stimulant

Uses: Air Disinfectant, Asthma, Bronchitis, Burns, Cuts, Decongestant, Flu, Headaches, Insect Repellent, Muscle Aches, Rheumatism, Sinusitis, Skin Ulcers, Urinary Infections, Wounds

Caution: Eucalyptus should not be used if you have high blood pressure or epilepsy and can be fatal if ingested.

Fennel

Effects: Clearing

Note: Middle note

Aroma: Sweet, Earthy

Combines with: Geranium, Lavender, Sandalwood

Properties: Antiseptic, Antispasmodic, Diuretic, Stimulant

Uses: Digestive Disorders, Gout (combine with Juniper), Nervous Tension

Caution: Do not use fennel during pregnancy or if you have epilepsy. Fennel may irritate sensitive skin.

Frankincense

Effects: Uplifting, Relaxing

Note: Note: Base/Middle note

Aroma: Sweet, Warm

Combines with: Lavender, Neroli, Rose

Properties: Analgesic, Antidepressant, Anti-inflammatory, Antiseptic, Expectorant

Uses: Asthma, Bronchitis, Colds, Healing Wounds, Tension, Respiratory Conditions, Skin Care (mature/aging skin), Uterine Tonic (can be used for heavy periods and massage following childbirth)

Caution: None

Geranium

Effects: Comforting, Healing

Note: Middle note

Aroma: Floral, Sweet, Earthy

Combines with: Chamomile, Cypress, Juniper

Properties: Antifungal, Antiseptic, Antispasmodic, Diuretic

Uses: Burns, Eczema, Oedema, Fluid Retention, Neuralgia, PMS Symptoms (including swollen breasts), Poor Circulation, Rheumatism, Tonsillitis

Caution: Geranium may irritate sensitive skin. Avoid use during pregnancy due to antispasmodic properties.

Ginger

Effects: Warming

Note: Top note

Aroma: Warm, Spicy, Woody

Combines with: Cedarwood, Citrus oils, Eucalyptus

Properties: Analgesic, Antidepressant, Expectorant, Stimulant

Uses: Arthritis, Bronchitis, Catarrh, Colds, Colic, Constipation, Diarrhoea, Exhaustion, Flatulence, Flu, Indigestion, Poor Circulation, Rheumatism, Sinusitis

Caution: Ginger may irritate sensitive skin.

Grapefruit

Effects: Refreshing

Note: Top note

Aroma: Sweet, Citrus

Combines with: Lavender, other Citrus oils

Properties: Antiseptic, Astringent, Diuretic, Stimulant

Uses: Anxiety, Depression, Digestive problems, Water Retention

Caution: Grapefruit is a photo sensitizer (increases the skins reaction to sunlight making it more likely to burn) so it should not be used when exposed to sunlight or tanning beds.

Hyssop

Effects: Stimulating

Note: Middle note

Aroma: Warm, Sweet

Combines with: Fennel, Lavender, Tangerine

Properties: Antiseptic, Antispasmodic, Astringent, Diuretic, Expectorant, Stimulant

Uses: Asthma, Bronchitis, Cold, Cough, Mental Tension, Sore Throat, Stomach Cramps, Water Retention

Caution: Hyssop should not be used during pregnancy, or if you have high blood pressure or epilepsy.

Jasmine

Effects: Soothing, Relaxing

Note: Base note

Aroma: Warm, Floral

Combines with: Chamomile, Citrus oils, Rose

Properties: Antidepressant, Antiseptic, Antispasmodic, Expectorant

Uses: Anxiety, Catarrh, Cough, Headache, Lack of Confidence, Laryngitis, Mental Tension, Sensitive or Dry Skin

Caution: Occasionally allergic reactions can occur. Jasmine should not be used during pregnancy because of its antispasmodic properties.

Lavender

Effects: Calming, Therapeutic

Note: Middle note

Aroma: Floral, Sweet, Woody, Herbal

Combines with: Clary Sage, Frankincense, Geranium

Properties: Analgesic, Anti-inflammatory, Antiseptic, Diuretic, Insecticide, Sedative

Uses: Acne, Anxiety, Bronchitis, Burns, Catarrh, Chilblains, Circulatory Problems, Colds, Dandruff, Eczema, Flu, Headaches, Insect Bites, Insomnia, Muscle Aches and Pains, PMS Symptoms, Psoriasis, Rheumatism, Sinusitis, Skin Problems, Sunburn, Tension, Throat Infection, Wounds and Sores

Caution: Lavender should not be used during the early stages of pregnancy. Use Lavender with caution if you have low blood pressure.

Lemon

Effects: Refreshing, Stimulating

Note: Top note

Aroma: Fresh, Sharp Citrus

Combines with: Chamomile, Lavender, Ylang Ylang

Properties: Antiseptic, Astringent, Antiviral, Stimulant

Uses: Cellulite, Chilblains, Circulatory Problems, Cold Sores, Constipation, Corns, Gingivitis, Headaches, Insect Bites, Migraine, Rheumatism, Sinusitis, Skin Tonic, Sore Throat, Tonsillitis, Varicose Veins

Caution: Should not be used when exposed to sunlight or tanning beds. Lemon should not be directly inhaled.

Lemongrass

Effects: Refreshing, Toning

Note: Top note

Aroma: Sweet, Citrus

Combines with: Basil, Cedarwood, Lavender

Properties: Antidepressant, Antiseptic, Diuretic

Uses: Colic, Fatigue, Indigestion, Muscle Aches and Pains, Stimulates Appetite, Stress

Caution: None

Marjoram

Effects: Soothing, Warming

Note: Middle note

Aroma: Warm, Spicy

Combines with: Bergamot, Cedarwood, Lavender

Properties: Analgesic, Antiseptic, Antispasmodic, Diuretic

Uses: Anxiety, Arthritis, Bronchitis, Bruises, Colic, Constipation, Digestive Problems, Flatulence, Insomnia, Muscle Aches and Pains, PMS Symptoms, Rheumatism, Sinusitis, Sprains

Caution: Marjoram has antispasmodic properties so do not use during pregnancy.

Melissa / Lemon Balm

Effects: Uplifting, Refreshing

Note: Middle note

Aroma: Fresh, Sweet, Herbal

Combines with: Bergamot, Eucalyptus, Geranium

Properties: Antidepressant, Antispasmodic, Sedative

Uses: Acne, Cold Sores, Colds, Cough, Flu, PMS Symptoms, Stress

Caution: Melissa / Lemon Balm may cause skin irritation. Use well diluted. Do not use during pregnancy.

Myrrh

Effects: Toning, Rejuvenating

Note: Middle note

Aroma: Warm, Spicy (similar to musk)

Combines with: Clove, Frankincense, Geranium

Properties: Analgesic, Antiseptic, Astringent, Expectorant

Uses: Arthritis, Bronchitis, Colds, Cough, Digestive Problems, Mouth and Gum Problems, Stimulates Immune System

Caution: Myrrh should not be used during pregnancy.

Neroli

Effects: Relaxing

Note: Top note

Aroma: Floral, Refreshing

Combines with: Chamomile, Lavender, Sandalwood

Properties: Antidepressant, Antiseptic, Antispasmodic, Sedative

Uses: Depression, Digestive Problems, Dry or Sensitive Skin, Flatulence, Headaches, Insomnia, Irritable Bowel Syndrome, Nervous Tension, Panic Attacks, Stress

Caution: Neroli has antispasmodic properties and should not be used during pregnancy.

Orange

Effects: Refreshing, Relaxing

Note: Top note

Aroma: Fresh, Citrus

Combines with: Frankincense, Lavender, Rosemary

Properties: Antidepressant, Antiseptic, Antispasmodic, Detoxifying, Sedative, Tonic

Uses: Anxiety, Cellulite, Constipation, Depression, Diarrhoea, Digestive Problems, Dry/Sensitive/Aging Skin, Flatulence, Indigestion, Insomnia, Muscle, Aches and Pains, Nervous Tension, Respiratory Conditions, Stress

Caution: Orange has antispasmodic properties and should not be used during pregnancy. Orange may irritate sensitive skin (use well diluted). Should not be used when exposed to sunlight or tanning beds.

Patchouli

Effects: Relaxing

Note: Base note

Aroma: Sweet, Spicy, Woody

Combines with: Geranium, Lavender, Neroli

Properties: Antidepressant, Anti-inflammatory, Antiseptic, Astringent, Diuretic, Sedative

Uses: Anxiety, Cellulite, Chapped/Cracked Skin, Depression, Eczema, Increase Libido, PMS Symptoms, Scar Tissue, Water Retention

Caution: None

Peppermint

Effects: Refreshing, Stimulating

Note: Top note

Aroma: Strong, Fresh, Menthol

Combines with: Eucalyptus, Lavender, Rosemary

Properties: Analgesic, Antiseptic, Antispasmodic, Astringent, Decongestant, Digestive Aid, Expectorant

Uses: Asthma, Bronchitis, Colic, Headaches, Indigestion, Insect Repellent, Migraine, Muscle and Joint Pain, Nausea, Sinusitis, Sore/Tired Feet, Toothaches

Caution: Peppermint has antispasmodic properties therefore do not use during pregnancy.

Pine

Effects: Refreshing, Stimulating

Note: Middle note

Aroma: Fresh, Woody

Combines with: Eucalyptus, Geranium, Lavender
Properties: Antiseptic, Decongestant, Disinfectant, Expectorant, Tonic
Uses: Bronchitis, Cystitis, Flu, Gout, Laryngitis, Muscle Aches and Pains, Respiratory Problems, Rheumatism, Sinusitis
Caution: Pine may cause skin irritation in sensitive skin.

Rose
Effects: Relaxing
Note: Base/Middle note
Aroma: Warm, Deep Floral
Combines with: Bergamot, Chamomile, Geranium
Properties: Antibacterial, Antidepressant, Antiseptic, Antispasmodic, Astringent, Diuretic, Sedative
Uses: Aging Skin, Broken Veins, Depression, Dry Skin, Headache, Insomnia, PMS Symptoms, Sensitive Skin, Sore Throat, Stress
Caution: Rose has antispasmodic properties and should not be used during pregnancy.

Rosemary
Effects: Refreshing, Stimulating
Note: Middle note
Aroma: Refreshing, Woody, Herbal
Combines with: Cedarwood, Geranium, Juniper
Properties: Analgesic, Antidepressant, Ant rheumatic, Antiseptic, Antispasmodic, Decongestant, Diuretic, Stimulant
Uses: Burns, Cellulite, Colds, Digestive Problems, Fatigue, Flu, Gout, Liver and Gall Bladder Problems, Oily Skin, Poor Circulation, Rheumatism, Water Retention, Wounds

Caution: Rosemary has antispasmodic properties and should not be used during pregnancy or if you have high blood pressure or epilepsy.

Sandalwood

Effects: Warming, Relaxing

Note: Base note

Aroma: Woody, Sweet, Exotic

Combines with: Frankincense, Geranium, Jasmine

Properties: Anti-inflammatory, Antiseptic, Antispasmodic, Aphrodisiac, Diuretic, Sedative

Uses: Anxiety, Bronchitis, Cystitis, Fatigue, Frigidity, Impotence, Immune System Booster, Nervous Tension, Skin Conditions (such as acne, dry skin, eczema), Sore Throat, Stress, Urinary Infections, Water Retention

Caution: Should not be used during pregnancy or during states of depression.

Tea Tree

Effects: Cleansing, Refreshing

Note: Top note

Aroma: Fresh, Medicinal

Combines with: Best to use on its own

Properties: Antibiotic, Antifungal, Antiseptic, Antiviral, Detoxifying, Insecticide, Stimulant

Uses: Age Spots, Athlete's Foot, Boils, Burns, Catarrh, Colds, Corns, Cystitis, Dandruff, Fungal Infections, Immune System Booster, Itching (from insect bites, chicken pox, etc.), Sunburn, Urinary Tract Infections, Warts

Caution: Tea Tree may irritate sensitive skin

Thyme

Effects: Refreshing, Warming

Note: Note: Top note

Aroma: Sweet, Strong, Herbal

Combines with: Bergamot, Cedarwood, Chamomile

Properties: Anti rheumatic, Antiseptic, Antispasmodic, Aphrodisiac, Diuretic, Expectorant

Uses: Arthritis, Colds, Cough, Depression, Immune System Booster, Fatigue, Laryngitis, Memory Enhancer, Raises Low Blood Pressure, Rheumatism, Sore Throat, Stress, Tonsillitis

Caution: Tea Tree has antispasmodic properties and should not be used during pregnancy or if you have high blood pressure. Avoid prolonged use as toxicity is possible.

Ylang Ylang

Effects: Relaxing, Stimulating

Note: Base/Middle note

Aroma: Heavy, Sweet, Floral, Exotic

Combines with: Cedarwood, Clary Sage, Geranium

Properties: Antidepressant, Antiseptic, Aphrodisiac, Sedative

Uses: Anxiety, High Blood Pressure, Intestinal Problems, Sexual Dysfunction, Stress

Caution: Ylang Ylang may irritate sensitive skin. Do not use on inflammatory skin conditions and dermatitis. Ylang Ylang has a strong aroma and may cause headaches.

Many thanks to

www.aworldofaromatherapy.com and www.aromaweb.com for providing information for this chapter.

4
REFLEXOLOY

The ancient origins of Reflexology are lost in the past, we do not know exactly when or where it began. Some form of foot massage was performed in ancient China, India and Egypt but we do not know exactly how far back they date. However, modern reflexology developed without the knowledge of these systems. The modern system began with the development of zone therapy by an American called Dr Fitzgerald. He qualified as a doctor and studied with interest the techniques of Dr H Bressler from Vienna who was researching ways of treating certain conditions with pressure points. This extract from the book *Zone Therapy* by Dr Fitzgerald and Dr Bowers, published in 1917, explains how Dr Fitzgerald discovered and developed his ideas:

'I accidentally discovered that pressure with a cotton tipped probe on the mucocutaneous margin of the nose gave an anaesthetic result as though a cocaine solution had been applied. I further found that there were many spots in the nose, mouth, throat, and on both surfaces of the tongue which, when pressed firmly, deadened definite areas of sensation. Also, that pressures exerted over any body eminence, on the hands, feet or over the joints, produced the same characteristic results in pain relief. I found also that when pain was relieved, the condition that produced the pain was most generally relieved. This lead to my 'mapping out' these various areas and their associated connections, and also to noting the conditions influenced through them. This science I have named zone therapy.'

A lady called Eunice Ingham is now widely regarded as the mother of modern Reflexology. Eunice spent many years researching and developing techniques, which transformed the fairly basic and unrefined methods of zone therapy in to the technically detailed healing practice we know today. Eunice discovered that the whole body could be mapped out through the reflexes on the feet, as if the feet were a mirror of the whole body. As the excellent results of her work continued word spread and people from miles around came to see her and receive treatments. Eunice's nephew, Dwight Byers, received many treatments for his asthma and hay fever and his aunt talked to him during those treatments about her work and how her research was developing. Today Dwight runs the International Institute of Reflexology.

There are no definitive explanations of how reflexology actually works. Many reflexologists believe that the feet and hands are linked to various parts of the body by a countless number of nerve connections. It is thought that the nerve endings correspond to the map of the human physiology. If we look at the soles of the left and right foot they appear to form the general shape of the human body with the big toes relating to the head and neck of the torso, the base of the little toes as the left and right shoulder, each instep as the left and right side of the spine and so on. A similar view can be developed for the hands with the spine running up the inside and the thumbs being the neck and head.

An alternative theory explains reflexology through the principals of Chinese medicine. This stipulates that within the body there are a number of invisible energy pathways or meridians that carry life force energy or Chi/Ki. Sometimes acupuncture or acupressure is used to release blockages and stimulate a free flow of healthy life force energy. As most of the major energy pathways end or begin in the feet so naturally reflexology will stimulate them in a similar way.

Obviously it can take many years to become an expert reflexologist but your treatments can be very effective right from the start. There are a few basic techniques that you need to learn in order to begin a treatment, you can practice these on your own hands and feet. Once you have become familiar with these you can begin to treat the reflexes on your own and others' feet. Don't be afraid to start treating friends and family as soon as you have some basic understanding of the simple techniques. You can do no harm and the sooner you start the sooner you will become accomplished and able to really help others.

There is a standard sequence of reflexes to treat in order to give a full treatment but you can do no harm by making up your own sequence. The main point to remember is simply use the reflexology massage techniques to cover all the reflex areas on each foot and if your patient has a known illness spend a little longer treating the reflexes that relate to that condition. Also you can show them where these reflexes are so that they can treat themselves. Just one word of warning, you can over-stimulate a reflex so only recommend that the patient massage particular reflex points for a few minutes once or twice per day between your massage sessions, which will probably be once per week. It is also important to remember that some reflexes will be sensitive so do not apply too much pressure until you know what is comfortable for the patient. Once you have learned the foot massage techniques you can use them with essential oils in the same way you use essential oils with a full body massage, but obviously you need much less oil. So take this in to account when you create a blend before the treatment.

FOOT MASSAGE TECHNIQUES

Giving a reflexology treatment will involve using your hands to apply pressure and different types of massage to the feet. The techniques are simple but require practice and patience to perfect them. Practice the basic techniques on your own hands or feet, this shows you how the techniques feel to the patient. You will also learn how much pressure to apply, which is important for the patient's comfort and saves the therapist's muscles from strain.

Treating the feet and performing the different types of hand movements do not require great strength. Although initially your shoulders, arms and hands may feel some strain before they become stronger, so it is helpful to pace yourself and not take on too much, perhaps just a few treatments per week as a start. Eventually you may be able to do several per day depending on your own strength, although quality is always better than quantity.

When you are treating others, be prepared to adapt to their needs. Some feet are very sensitive, and if the patient is ill and has never had reflexology before, the first few treatments may need to be very light. Some parts of the feet may be much more sensitive than others, so again, the first treatment should be a gentle exploration, noting those areas that need a lighter touch. This also helps to recognize progress in the treatment, when sensitive areas become less painful, this is a good sign that the corresponding physical anatomy is reacting well to the treatment.

Although deep massage can be applied using techniques like the knuckle press, you should only use them when you have gained enough experience. You should never use deep massage if the patient experiences pain, although a little discomfort is sometimes acceptable if the patient is genuinely accepting of this. Once you learn when to apply more pressure, these deep massage techniques can be very effective when used sparingly. Again, never use deep foot massage in the first or second treatment of a new client unless you are sure it is wise to do so!

You can cover a reflex area two or three times until you are satisfied it has been properly treated, although over-stimulation of reflexes is to be avoided, especially in the very ill, children, pregnant women, particularly sensitive people, and those patients coming for their first or second treatment. Some reflexologists always use a very light touch, and this is also an effective technique. It certainly helps the patient to relax and seems to induce a subtle yet deep state of healing, particularly helpful for patients with mental and emotional problems. As an individual therapist, you need to practice and find your own way of doing things, the way that naturally feels right to you is usually the best and most effective. There is no reason not to use a different technique with different types of patients according to their needs and your experience and confidence.

This section explains the basic reflexology techniques. These are the most important techniques to learn and are used often throughout a treatment. They are not difficult to master with a little practice, and as mentioned the best place to practice at first is simply on your own hands or feet.

SUPPORTING THE FOOT

This basic support hold is used often throughout a treatment. While one hand is working a particular set of reflexes, the other hand is always used to support the foot, a firm but gentle grip prevents the foot from moving around too much. Hold the top of the patient's foot, with your fingers on top of the toes and your thumb on the ball of the foot. For best results, when working on reflexes on the inside of the patient's right foot, use

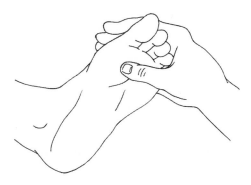

your right hand as the support. When working on the outside of the foot, use your left hand as the support. This pattern is then reversed to work on the left foot. Make sure not to bend the toes forward and do not stretch the foot too far in any direction. Remember, the patient's comfort is always paramount. Other support grips can be used, for example 'cupping' the back of the heel with one hand whilst your other hand is used to massage the reflexes.

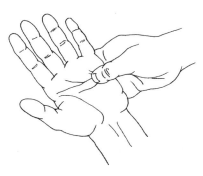

FINGER OR THUMB WALKING TECHNIQUE

This massage technique is one of the most basic and often-used through-out a treatment. Again, the best way to practice the motion and gauge the level of pressure is on your own hand. Support the back of one hand with the fingers of the other hand. Gently press the thumb into the palm. Release the pressure slowly while at the same time sliding the thumb forward slightly then apply gentle pressure again. Keep repeating this.

The main point is that there should be no gaps or spaces between the pressure points so that not even the smallest area of the reflex is missed. The action should be repeated constantly while trying to move in a straight line across the palm. The whole movement is a sort of rhythmic nibbling action. If you are right-handed, you will probably find it easier to use your right thumb, but with practice you will be able to use both thumbs as easily. This is important as both hands are used equally during a full treatment. This same nibbling or walking massage action is used with the fingers. This is usually performed with the index finger alone or the index and second finger together. Some reflexologists like to combine the finger and thumb walking movements with a small rotating motion, so that as pressure is applied, you move the thumb in a tiny circular motion, usually clockwise, this is repeated with every move forward. You might like this technique and find it simple to use and very effective. However, if you find it difficult, just use the normal technique to begin with.

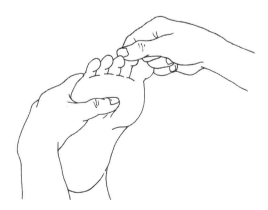

FINGER AND THUMB MASSAGE

This technique is a simple rubbing or massaging action. The above diagram shows the index finger being used to massage the top and side of a toe. The thumb helps to support the toe, the other hand is employed in the basic support bold. Simply rub the index finger back and forth - some reflexologists use an additional circular motion, so you can use this if it feels right. You can also practice this technique on your hands.

The two-finger massage technique, shown below, uses the index and second fingers to massage the top of the foot (which is the reflex for the pelvic area, reproductive organs, and lymphatic system). The technique used is similar to finger or thumb walking, although a circular motion is also employed as the fingers "nibble" along. Some reflexologists remove the nibble action here and simply use the circular massage action.

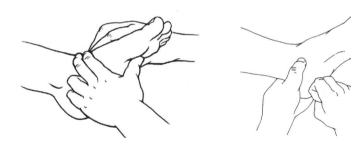

PRESSURE TECHNIQUE

There are two types of massage used here. The first involves gently pinching and holding the heel with the thumb and index finger, this is the pressure technique. The second type uses one or two knuckles to knead a particular area, as shown above. A little more pressure is usually applied to the heel area as it is often covered by toughened skin, and the reflexes are located a little deeper. The knuckle can be pressed in and dragged down, or pressed in and gently rotated, moving slightly and pressed and rotated again, and so on. Alternatively a kneading action can be used, as though you were kneading bread. You can work from left to right or top to bottom, as long as the whole heel area is covered.

PRESSURE POINT HOLD

Some reflexologists find that certain areas of the feet respond well to a simple pressure hold. A need for this might be indicated by skin that seems limp, puffy or lacking 'energy'. Treat the centre of this kind of area by applying pressure with your thumb or knuckle. The pressure should be no more than is comfortable for the patient, and should last between five to ten seconds, occasionally longer, and can be repeated two or three times during the treatment. This pressure point can correspond to a place in the body where life force energy is blocked or unbalanced. These blockages can sometimes move quite quickly when this pressure technique is applied. The patient may feel some sudden changes, movement within the body, tingling sensations, becoming more relaxed, etc. The therapist may also feel things change, and even the atmosphere in the room might feel different in a very short period of time. If anything unpleasant is experienced, do not over stimulate this point, carry on with the normal treatment and things will settle down quickly. You can come back to the same point later or in another treatment.

As mentioned all the above techniques need to be practiced as much as possible on your own hands and feet, or on the feet of family or friends. Remember, you can do no harm with reflexology. It is a perfectly safe technique to use if you always follow the instructions and use a light massage technique until you have gained some experience. In a full treatment you can follow the sequence of reflexes as they are numbered in the diagrams below or you can develop your own sequence. Don't worry as accuracy is not so important, as long as you feel you have covered all the reflex points with the massage techniques that feel effective to you. You can spend extra time on specific reflexes where you know the patient needs help. You can then start to apply your own experience and creativity to improve the techniques.

REFLEX DIAGRAMS

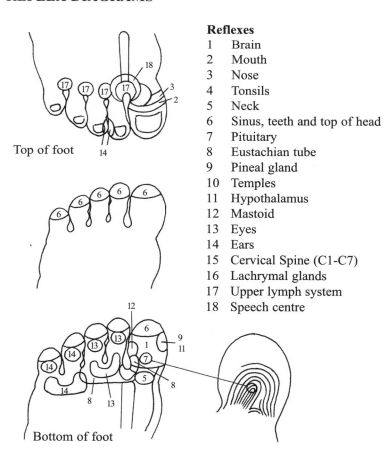

Reflexes
1   Brain
2   Mouth
3   Nose
4   Tonsils
5   Neck
6   Sinus, teeth and top of head
7   Pituitary
8   Eustachian tube
9   Pineal gland
10 Temples
11 Hypothalamus
12 Mastoid
13 Eyes
14 Ears
15 Cervical Spine (C1-C7)
16 Lachrymal glands
17 Upper lymph system
18 Speech centre

Top of foot

Bottom of foot

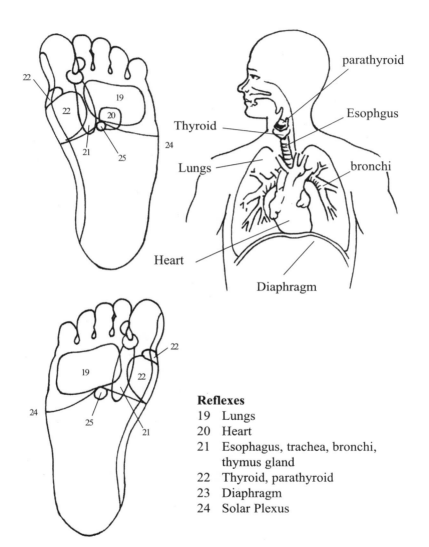

Reflexes
19 Lungs
20 Heart
21 Esophagus, trachea, bronchi,
    thymus gland
22 Thyroid, parathyroid
23 Diaphragm
24 Solar Plexus

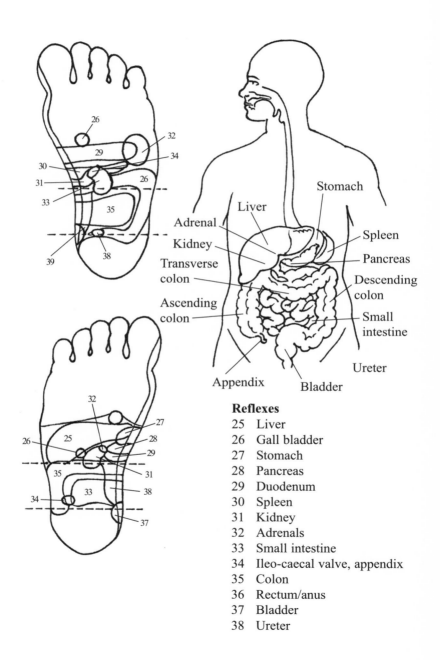

Reflexes

25 Liver
26 Gall bladder
27 Stomach
28 Pancreas
29 Duodenum
30 Spleen
31 Kidney
32 Adrenals
33 Small intestine
34 Ileo-caecal valve, appendix
35 Colon
36 Rectum/anus
37 Bladder
38 Ureter

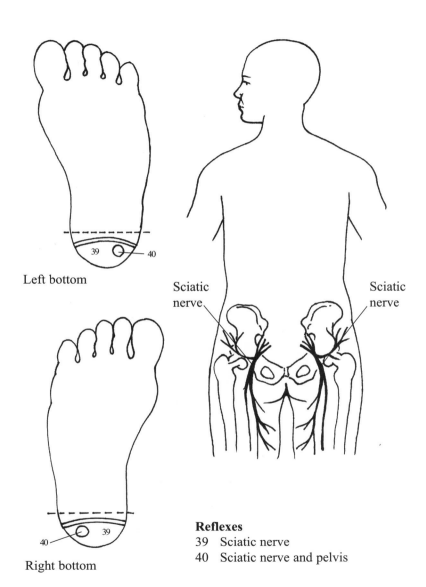

Left bottom

Right bottom

Sciatic nerve

Sciatic nerve

Reflexes

39 Sciatic nerve
40 Sciatic nerve and pelvis

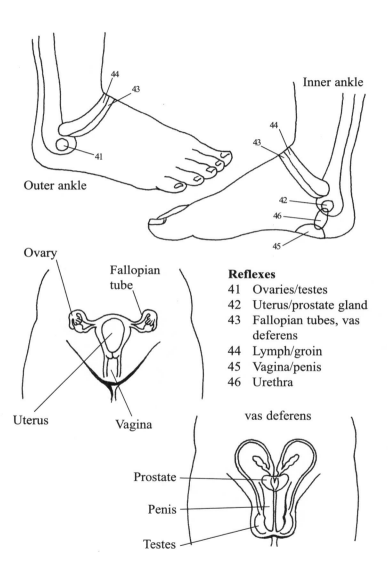

44
43
41
Outer ankle

Inner ankle
44
43
42
46
45

Ovary

Fallopian tube

Uterus

Vagina

Reflexes
41 Ovaries/testes
42 Uterus/prostate gland
43 Fallopian tubes, vas deferens
44 Lymph/groin
45 Vagina/penis
46 Urethra

vas deferens

Prostate

Penis

Testes

Reflexes
47 Knee
48 Hip
49 Elbow
50 Shoulder

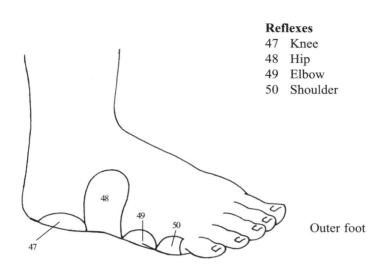

Outer foot

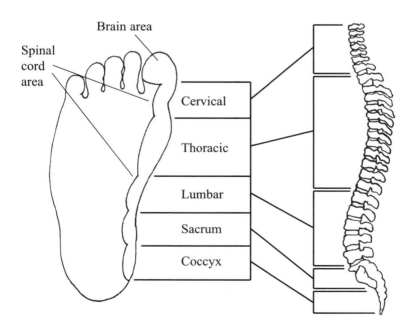

Reflexes

2   Mouth
3   Nose
4   Tonsils
16   Lachrymal glands (tear ducts)
17   Upper lymph system
18   Speech center
44   Fallopian tubes, vas deferens
45   Lymph/groin
52   Breast
53   Circulation

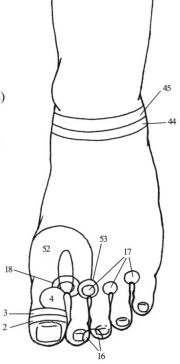

5
REIKI

Nowadays many people have heard of Reiki. It will soon be as well known as other mainstream complementary therapies like reflexology and aromatherapy. Dr Mikao Usui was the founder of Reiki in its present form, he was a Buddhist monk living in Japan in the last century. Dr Usui had a keen interest in the healing arts and sciences and he had a great passion to relieve the suffering of others, especially the sick. It was this drive coupled with his understanding of the body and mind that led him on a fascinating journey to  discover a simple method of healing body and mind that anyone could practice successfully.

Reiki is a simple system of hands-on healing but it can also be used as a powerful path to personal and spiritual growth. Reiki can have a profound effect on health and well-being by rebalancing, cleansing and renewing our subtle internal energy system. When a Reiki practitioner places her or his hands on or near the patient there is an immediate flow or transfer of 'healing energy'. This is a wonderful thing to experience, very peaceful, very calming and very natural. During a full Reiki treatment the practitioner will place their hands in about twelve different positions on or near the front and back of the body and this might last up to an hour.

This healing energy is Reiki or Universal Life Force Energy as it is translated from Japanese. It could also be called Universal Chi or Ki. Life

Force Energy is the basic force of life without it nothing would exist. There is an abundance of this pure energy in the countryside or by the sea. But in built up areas this natural life giver is often restricted or of poor quality, however there are many ways we can combat this. Apart from giving/receiving Reiki one way is to regularly and consistently think positively and compassionately and practice contentment. This naturally improves our internal Chi and helps to ward off ill health and obviously unhappiness. A good way to develop these inner qualities is to learn some simple meditation techniques.

Some people see Reiki as a very pure form of subtle energy. When it is introduced to the body it naturally removes energy blockages and purifies or raises the quality of our own internal energies. Often the immediate effects of this are more energy, feeling relaxed and being able to deal with the daily hassles of life with a positive mind. But there is also often a feeling of coming home to yourself and becoming more aware that you are much more than just a physical and mental being. The presence of Reiki serves to reconnect us to our divinity, our true nature. It can bring us to a fresh awareness of ourselves and help us see our lives and the world around us in a new light. These changes can be very subtle and it is often others who point them out and say things like, 'You seem different' or 'You seem more relaxed and at peace'! There is definitely a sense of increased contentment and peace of mind with those who practice or receive Reiki. This understanding fits in with an alternative translation from the Japanese which states that Reiki is 'spiritually guided life force energy'. This hints that Reiki is a little more than just life force energy, as if there is some thing else behind it or with it. We do not know what this is as Reiki has no doctrine or religion. Perhaps we could say Reiki is some kind of healing blessing or some expression of a universal force for good. A suitable explanation is not too important as Reiki is very much an experiential technique, it has great power to help people whatever their background or beliefs.

One of the unusual qualities of Reiki is that anyone can become a Reiki practitioner in just one or two days. All we need to do is find a Reiki teacher that we feel comfortable with and then take the First Degree course. This will teach you how to treat yourself and others. The main focal point of the course is the attunements or empowerments that open and expand your capacity to channel Reiki. This is a wonderful experience for many people and is often the beginning of a lifelong journey towards better health and personal happiness.

However we all carry Reiki, even without taking the special Reiki attunements. Most healthy people have a very strong life force energy which they can use to heal others just through the power of touch. You can feel your own life force energy. Sit quietly for a few minutes with your hands resting in your lap, palms up. Focus your mental awareness on the centre of each palm, you might already begin to feel something! Then hold your hands out in front so that your palms are facing each other, almost as if you are holding an imaginary ball, bring your hands together very slowly and you will start to feel a cushion of energy, this is Chi or life force energy. Another way to feel this is to point the fingers of one hand at the palm of the other so that they are just a few centimetres apart, close your eyes and gently move the hand that is pointing. You will begin to feel a gentle tingling sensation in your palm.

There are many accounts of how effective Reiki is in combating illness and improving quality of life. We can use Reiki as a simple but very effective healing technique but in the greater context Reiki also gives us the opportunity to broaden our internal horizons, expand our spiritual awareness and finally find some true peace of mind. Because

Reiki is energy and energy follows intention we can use Reiki in many ways to improve our life and help others. Here are a few examples of the many ways you can use Reiki through touch or simply by setting clear mental intentions:

For personal growth, healing deep-seated personal issues and developing compassion, empathy, wisdom, patience and other good inner qualities

To heal animals and plants

To heal relationship problems at work or home

To send healing energy to world situations such as wars and natural disasters, or local situations such as crime, unemployment and poverty

To complement and strengthen other therapies such as Aromatherapy, Reflexology, Counselling etc.

To find new employment, a new house, car, or anything else!

To have a safe and swift journey while travelling

To find a solution to a specific problem

To calm yourself before going into stressful situations such as exams, interviews or public speaking

To always be blessed, guided, and protected

There are so many ways we can use Reiki, the only limitations are our imagination and faith. By developing the courage to let go and experience the true essence of Reiki we can begin to realise our true nature as a whole and healthy physical, mental and spiritual being. Learning Reiki can become the first step on a very enjoyable and enlightening journey towards realising our true potential, whatever we perceive that to be.

Although we need to receive an authentic 'attunement' from a Reiki teacher in order to practice fully we can practice Reiki just using the level of life force energy that we possess now. Also we can increase the quality of our Reiki by living a healthy and spiritual life. If we have a healthy diet, practice regular meditation and prayer and do some energy exercise like yoga, Tai Chi or Chi Gung or just enjoy walks in the countryside all these things will help us to carry more powerful Reiki. One very nice way to start this process is to go somewhere that you know is a special place, maybe high on a mountain or by a quiet lake or stream or just sit with your back to a large tree or visit a church or temple that you feel has a special energy. Spend some quiet time there just relaxing and soaking up the good energy and then make a special request or intention, 'from this time on I would like to carry a special healing energy that I can use to help others' say this three times and then gently focus on the words 'healing energy' for as long as you feel is right.

Once you have done this you can start to practice Reiki in your own way. Simply put your hands on or near your own body or the person you want to treat and the healing energy will begin to flow to where it is most needed. For a full treatment use the following hand positions, stay in each position for a few minutes then move to the next without losing contact with the body. You can stay in one position for longer if you feel that extra healing is needed in that area. These are the basic Reiki hand positions, but you can give Reiki in other ways for example just by spending time listening to someone who needs to talk. They will naturally soak up your healing energy; we do not always have to touch the person who needs help. Also you can send someone Reiki with your thoughts just by visualising it happening or just setting the mental intention. Dr Usui also taught other ways to give Reiki using the breath and even by just using the eyes; you can send someone Reiki just by looking at them, although these techniques require some awareness of energy and are probably best acquired from an experienced teacher. In the Western Reiki tradition there are three or four levels of practice and if you want to progress through these and increase your ability to heal others you will need to find a good Reiki teacher. As mentioned we can practice Reiki just by developing and using our own natural level of life force energy, however, the empowerments we can receive from an experienced Reiki teacher can make a big difference to our capacity to heal our self and others.

HAND POSITIONS FOR SELF TREATMENT

Eyes

With your fingers and thumbs together place your palms lightly over your eyes, so you can see no light if you open your eyes. Do not touch your eyes or restrict breathing by pressing on your nose.

Temples

In this position your palms should be over your temples, with your fingers and thumbs pointing toward the crown of your head.

Base of Skull

Slide your hands to the base of your skull to the occipital bone (bony lump). Your hands can overlap or stay side-by-side in this position as long as the occipital bone is covered.

Neck and Throat

Bring your hands down to your neck so the base of each palm or wrist touches your throat and the rest of your palms and fingers wrap gently around your neck.

Heart

Slide the hands down to the top of the chest, about the level of the heart, so that they are horizontally flat against your chest. The fingertips of each hand should touch lightly

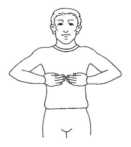

Solar Plexus

Again, keeping contact with the body, move your hands down so that your palms rest on the bottom of your ribcage and your fingers meet directly over the solar plexus, which is directly below the centre of your ribcage.

Navel

In this position your fingertips should touch gently about an inch below the navel, with your hands still horizontal, if it is comfortable.

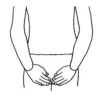

Groin

Move your hands down so that they fit into the natural V-shape in the groin. Your fingertips should just touch.

Top of Shoulders

Slide your hands up the front of the body, without losing contact, and round your neck so that your fingers touch the top of the spine. Move your hands as far down the back as is comfortable, your hands will form a V-shape.

Below Shoulder Blades

Bring your right hand to the top of your left shoulder and move the left hand so that your palm is flat against the base of your right shoulder blade. Repeat this the other way round. If you cannot manage this, simply repeat the front position.

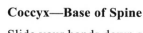

Small of Back

In this position, your hands should be at about the level of your navel, again as horizontal as possible.

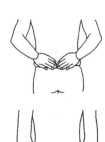

Coccyx—Base of Spine

Slide your hands down so that your fingers touch and are level with the tip of your tailbone.

HAND POSITIONS FOR TREATING OTHERS

Eyes

Sit behind your patient's head for the first four positions. Place your hands together over or just touching the face, so that your palms are over their eyes eyes, but not restricting breathing through their nose.

Temples

Lightly move your hands to the side of the head so your palms are over the temples and the thumbs touch in the center of the forehead. Alternatively place your palms over the ears and keep your fingers and thumbs together.

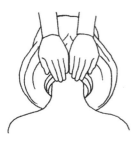

Base of Skull

Slowly move their head to one side so that one hand is carrying the weight of the head while you slide the other hand under the base of the skull. Gently roll the head onto the hand at the base of the skull and slide the free hand around to meet it so that the head is cradled and straight.

Neck and Throat

Reverse the above procedure for removing the hands. Bring your hands around to each side of the neck so that your fingers touch over the centre of the throat. Your hands should gently

touch or be just off the neck and throat.

Heart

Stand up and move to one side of the patient while still retaining some contact with the body. Place your hands one in front of the other across the heart area, so that the fingertips of the nearest hand touch the base of the other palm in the centre of the body.

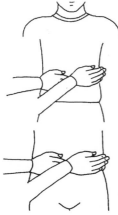

Solar Plexus

Move the hands down to the solar plexus area, just below the centre of the breastbone.

Navel

Slide the hands down to just below the navel area.

Groin

Lift the hands off the body in this position, unless you are treating someone you know well, and position them so that they form a V-shape over the groin area. Spend a few minutes giving Reiki to the knees and feet before asking the client to slowly turn over.

Top of Shoulders

Try to retain some contact with the body as the client is turning over and when they are settled bring the hands to the tops of the shoulders so they are in line. Alternatively, you can do this position lower, in line with the heart.

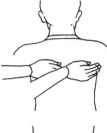

Shoulder Blades / Heart

This position corresponds to the solar plexus area, about halfway down the back.

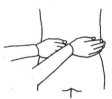

Waist

This position should be level with, or just below, the navel at about the waistline.

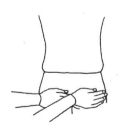

Coccyx

Slide your hands down so that they are about level with the end of the tailbone. Only touch this area if you are treating someone you know well. To finish the treatment spend a few minutes giving Reiki to the patient's knees and feet.

There are many fascinating aspects to Reiki. If you want to know more read *Reiki for Beginners* (Llewellyn) or *Reiki Mastery* (O Books) both by David Vennells or to find a Reiki teacher contact one of the organisations listed in the appendix.

6
THE BACH FLOWER REMEDIES

The Bach Flower remedies were developed during the 1930s by Dr Edward Bach, a medical doctor and a homeopath who lived and worked in England. He wanted to develop a simple and powerful system of natural medicine that anyone could practice; the remedies he discovered are now used all over the world. Originally conceived as remedies to cure illness they can also be used to support the process of spiritual development and personal growth. We could also say that using the remedies is a form of preventative medicine; they promote positive thoughts and emotions which naturally encourage and support mental and physical health. Many medical studies have shown the benefits of a positive outlook on the immune system, on the body's ability to recover from illness and injury and on the ability to cope with and recover from stressful events.

Through his early study and research Dr Bach became aware that to find a truly effective form of healing that would strike at the root of ill-health he would have to understand the true causes of illness. This led him in a similar direction to Samuel Hahnemann, the founder of homeopathy, and to the idea that illness is not simply a physical phenomena but mental in origin. The physical symptoms of disease are simply an external manifestation of inner dis-ease.

Being convinced that the root of physical illness lay within the mind Dr Bach knew that he would have to discover remedies that would work on the subtle mental and emotional levels of the mind, he would have to find remedies that were able to dispel negative states of mind and promote positive ones. These remedies would have to be specific enough to target the particular negative states of mind that were giving rise to the physical symptoms. He must have realised from homeopathy that the patient's state of mind could be improved when the appropriate remedy was prescribed and this would often give rise to good physical health. Both Bach and Hanhemann were men of great wisdom and their discoveries and philosophies were way ahead of their time and still way ahead of modern psychology and medicine. Both their systems of medicine have achieved incredible results and have brought great benefit to countless people.

Dr Bach wanted his remedies to be so easy to prescribe and use that anyone could take them without professional advice. The system he developed is very simple yet goes right to the heart of the problem. Imagine for example that you are suffering from asthma. There is no Bach Flower Remedy for asthma, since this is a physical complaint, instead you need to ignore the asthma and look at the kind of person you are. Perhaps you are someone who is shy and timid, and who gets nervous about things like speaking in public and meeting new people. This would indicate that you are a Mimulus type, so this would be the first remedy to select. Perhaps your son is about to start school and you are frightened that he will be bullied. Red Chestnut is the remedy for the fear that something bad will happen to loved ones. Perhaps you have been working too hard and are mentally exhausted; this would indicate the need for Olive. If your physical condition, is related to any of these inner problems then the remedy will relieve the illness once the inner problem is healed.

Whatever mental, emotional or physical condition we want to treat all we have to do is identify which states of mind predominate and choose the appropriate remedies accordingly. We do not need to have any knowledge of anatomy, physiology or be able to diagnose physical or mental illness because we are not treating ourselves or others in this way. We only need to be able to recognise our own states of mind or simply ask others how they are feeling!

If we are treating others on a regular basis we need to be sure that they are seeing a medical doctor if they have any serious conditions and we should never try to replace conventional treatment or medicines with the Bach remedies or any other complementary therapy. The Bach remedies will work in harmony with any conventional therapy and will not give any adverse side effects. They are very gentle healing agents and there is never the possibility of overdose, addiction or adverse effects from wrong diagnosis. They are perfectly pure and natural remedies and contain little or none of the original physical plant or tree, only the healing life force energy held within water and a little alcohol for preservation.

If we are diagnosing for ourselves and others and we have some knowledge of the remedies it is an easy task to choose the appropriate ones for use. Simply identify the main states of mind that are present i.e. anger, fear, indecision, etc. Make a note of all the remedies that are relevant, then try to put the symptoms in order of severity so that you have a list of possible remedies to use in order of importance. It should not be difficult to keep this list to within five or ten, this helps us to identify which remedies are most likely to be successful, then we can choose the remedies we want to try from this list.

Remember we are not treating a physical illness. So if someone is experiencing a strained ligament for example we should not choose a remedy for people who tend to over exert themselves. We should try to establish what sort of person they are, how they think and feel about themselves and the world around them, what is their character and disposition? For example are they dominant and controlling? Do they get angry easily, are they shy, are they constantly distracted or dreamy? We need to have a good knowledge of the remedies to spot these mental traits in our selves and others then we will begin to diagnose accurately and quickly.

There is no easy way to learn the 38 remedies, everyone has a different way of remembering things that work for them. One good way is to set yourself a target by trying to remember say two or three commonly used remedies each day, then within two or three weeks you will have a basic knowledge of all the remedies. Just try to remember the key words at first, shown at the beginning of each of the remedy descriptions that follow. When we have this basic knowledge we can really begin to get to know the remedies by using them as much as possible. The real key to success is developing the skill to recognise the relevant and predominant states of mind that someone is naturally disposed to or that accompany a particular illness.

We all tend to have a 'type remedy'. The type remedy is one or occasionally two remedies that make up the core or major traits of our personality. For example it is easy to spot someone who is always impatient, quick in thought and action and doesn't suffer fools gladly, their type remedy would be Impatiens! Also people who are dreamy, in a world of their own, are classic Clematis types. We can learn a lot about human nature in this way and we can do this kind of study and research anywhere, anytime and no one has to know that we are practising our diagnostic techniques!

So generally speaking when we are preparing a remedy we should try to identify the type remedy/remedies and then add whatever other remedies are relevant for the more short term or easily changeable states of mind. For example someone might be a Water Violet type; that is proud, aloof, quiet, likes being alone, often intelligent and artistic but during illness they may also experience constant and repetitive worrying thoughts that go round and round in their mind so this would also indicate White Chestnut. So we would use both remedies together, the White Chestnut being a more temporary remedy.

In choosing the final number of remedies we should be able to keep the number to within six or seven, often just a few remedies or just one is needed. Use your own judgement and intuition, then with experience you will become a skilled and accomplished healer. Also using too many remedies together can confuse the picture and we will not know which remedies are working and which are unnecessary.

Another good way to remember the remedies is to read briefly through all the remedy descriptions and make a note of those which are relevant to our own personality and the people we know well. Then buy these remedies and use them on yourself and others. We might need a good friend to help us spot our own type remedy, someone who knows us well and is not afraid to be honest with us!

After prescribing for yourself and a friend have a review session in two or three weeks time and share your experiences. You may find that some remedies have gone straight to the heart of the matter or you may decide to try others. Another useful idea is to keep a diary of your states of mind over a couple of weeks. Write down how you feel about yourself, your life and how you react to certain situations that arise. This can be a very useful way to recognise your predominant states of mind and those that are more fleeting and less deep seated, then tailor your remedy accordingly.

The key to successfully prescribing for others is simply learning to listen well. Let the other person guide the diagnosis. Try not to be too intrusive, help them to feel relaxed and secure and they will be open with you, don't try too hard to prise them open! Also it doesn't matter if we get the diagnosis wrong on the first or second attempt, all the Bach remedies have remarkable healing qualities and even the 'wrong' remedy can have good results!

If we intend to treat people on a regular basis a good knowledge and understanding of counselling skills can be very useful. Just learning to listen without judgement is an invaluable part of the healing process. It creates an environment that helps the patient relax and feel more able to talk openly about their problems. We can learn these skills from a good book and simply practice with family or friends or we can take a short course at a local college, there are many available nowadays. Learning to listen also helps us develop our ability to 'tune in' to others, their feelings, thoughts and personal characteristics. Listening also helps us to reduce our sense of self-importance which can create a mental barrier that prevents a clear and healthy patient/healer relationship. If we think other people are important we are obviously going to treat them with respect and kindness.

If we want to treat a short-term negative state of mind we simply put two drops of the remedy in a small glass of still water and sip it at intervals until our symptoms have improved. At night we can keep it by our bed and sip it during the night if we wake up; again we can combine a few remedies in one glass. We can drop the remedies straight on to our tongue; however still mineral water seems to work best as a 'carrier' of the healing life force. If we don't have mineral water available, boiled and cooled or filtered water will also work well and also fruit juice and normal tap water is fine if nothing else is available.

If we have a short-term illness like a cold, a minor injury or some sort of short-term emotional upset or worry like depression or shock we can choose remedies that will relieve our symptoms and help the healing process. Again we try to establish the predominant states of mind that accompany the problem and choose the appropriate remedy. For example, someone with a cold might be feeling very lazy, apathetic with no interest in anything and no wish to help themselves, they might also be feeling very despondent and want to be on their own and yet feel lonely. So this would indicate Wild Rose, Gentian and Water Violet.

Someone else with the same virus might be pushing and straining to carry on, they may also feel vulnerable and weak and these symptoms would indicate Vervain and Centaury. So both people need different remedies to get the best healing results even though they have the same illness. If these states of mind are brought on only during illness then using the right remedies can produce a swift recovery and we can administer the remedies as mentioned above, either in a glass of water or directly on to the tongue. The regularity of dosage is important, there is no danger of side effects, but there is no point taking more than you need.

If we want to treat more long-term mental or physical conditions ideally we need some clean 30ml dropper bottles, these can usually be obtained from a chemist, drug store or herbal supplier. Simply choose which remedies you want to use, put two or three drops from each stock bottle in to the empty dropper bottle and fill this with still mineral water. The minimum dosage is then four drops on the tongue four times a day and this should then last for about ten days or two weeks. Hold the remedy on the tongue for a short time before swallowing but try to avoid touching the dropper with your tongue if possible. We can take more than four drops four times a day if we feel we need to. A teaspoon of brandy can be added to the remedy bottle to keep it fresh. This is especially useful if it is not practical to keep the bottle in a fridge or we are using tap water, instead of mineral or spring water which tends to stay fresh for longer.

Once you have prepared the remedy it is best to keep it in a cool place and out of direct sunlight for any length of time. When the bottle is finished sterilise it and flush it out once or twice with spring water before reusing. If you do use brandy and are preparing the remedies for others then it is important to be aware that some people may be sensitive to alcohol or may not be able to take it for religious reasons. So they must be made aware that even the stock bottles that you buy over the counter contain a small amount of alcohol for its preservative qualities. The only way to overcome this would be to make the actual stock bottle yourself by preparing the remedy from the appropriate plant. This is a wonderful thing to do if you have the time and access to the right plants and trees. The methods for doing this can be found on the internet.

Taking at least four doses per day serves to steadily flood the body and mind with the appropriate type of healing life force energy. The effectiveness of this constant supply of healing energy gains momentum the longer and more consistently we take the remedies and over a few weeks we can see remarkable results. Sometimes it may take longer, perhaps six weeks or two months, especially if the illness has been a long one, but still if we persist with the treatment there can be a sudden improvement after several weeks of apparently little change. Perhaps this is because the healing energy needs time to build up in the system before it reaches a level that tips the balance towards good health.

Another way of taking the remedies is to buy a small bottle of still spring water and, put 6-8 drops of the remedies you need into the bottle. Turn the bottle over a few times to mix the remedy. Keep this bottle in the fridge or some other cool place out of direct sunlight and sip a small amount of this water 4-6 times a day, more if required, remember to hold the remedy on your tongue for a while before swallowing.

To remember to take the remedy at least four times a day it can be helpful to take it upon waking, after or before lunch, after or before your evening meal and just before you go to sleep. If you can spare the time whilst taking the remedy sit quietly or lie down for a few minutes whilst the healing energy that accompanies the remedy enters your system. Try to relax and switch off and mentally connect and open up to the healing energy. We may actually feel this as a spiral of energy coming from above or as a cushion of energy around the body. This sensation may wear off after a few minutes or it may stay with us for some time. The longer we take the remedies the more we may become aware of this healing energy around us, we may feel our mind become clearer and we may feel more relaxed, less stressed and more energised.

Some people may experience an emotional release connected with the healing process. This might be the result of some suppressed emotional response from years ago, a recent shock or accident, or it might be the release of accumulated stress gathered over the course of a long illness or through difficult life experiences. This is a good sign that the remedies are doing their job and helping us work towards inner and outer health. This release may also take the form of laughing a lot or any other sort of emotional expression. Obviously this can have an effect upon those around us, so if we are beginning to find our 'voice' for the first time and we want to express strong emotions we have to be careful and wise in our actions! Often these strong emotions, if they arise at all, are only passing phases and it is often advisable to just to watch them and allow them to 'come through' remembering that they will simply pass in time.

When taking the remedy we can think positive thoughts and

affirmations like, 'every day I am becoming more whole, happy and healthy' or we could say a short prayer and ask for healing blessings. We could do a short visualisation like imagining a spiral of pure healing energy entering our body and mind and renewing our health and vitality. We could see this energy as white, gold, deep blue, emerald green or any other colour that we feel is healing for us. We could visualise ourselves as relaxed, peaceful, healthy, happy and positive. Simple, childlike faith is the key to successful visualisation. Remember when you were a child and imagined being someone or something, maybe a doctor or some animal, when you played these roles you probably just really enjoyed believing you were that person. This is a powerful way to use our mind to encourage good health and a positive outlook. Simply visualise the kind of person you would like to be, enjoy and believe you are that person. Since our minds work through familiarity the more we do this the more it will become our reality.

These methods may not be suitable for everyone so we have to use our own judgement and experience to know when to use them or recommend them to others. Our mind can also get bored with the same visualisation, especially if we have been told we have to do it for a few weeks. For visualisations and affirmations to be effective they have to be of great interest and relevance to the individual, they have to be creative and evolve and change with the healing process.

It is worth remembering that Dr Bach had great faith in his remedies, he believed that if the patient truly and deeply wanted to be well the remedies would bring this about. This confidence in the power of the remedies is very important if we are prescribing them for others. The remedies have great healing potential but if we can support and encourage the patient's confidence in the remedies through our own natural belief then this can really make a positive difference to our healing practice. Often the patients who make the greatest effort from their own side stand the best chance of recovery. So if we can also encourage people not to worry and to be positive and to help themselves in whatever way they can then this can also add momentum to the healing process.

If many remedies are indicated for a treatment we can either choose those that are most important and relevant at present or use them all at once to provide a complete healing picture. If we choose the latter we can remove the less important remedies from the combination as healing takes place and they are no longer required. We can also add new ones each time we prepare a new remedy as the healing process sometimes throws up states of mind that were not obvious at first. It is worth remembering that two or three remedies that go right to the heart of the matter can be more effective than five or six. Accurate diagnosis and confidence in your choice is the key to success.

Generally we treat children in the same way we would treat adults, simply by prescribing according to their mental and emotional state. Children often respond very positively to the remedies, as do animals, and healing can often be swifter. Consequently we may need to change the remedy combination more quickly than normal. The obvious difference in treating young children and animals is that they cannot easily express their feelings clearly; however mood is often displayed through behaviour. Common emotions like anger, fear, shyness, etc can be recognised easily and we often only have to spend a little time watching how children play, how they react to meeting people and how they behave when they are unhappy. Like adults, when children and animals are ill their common states of mind may give way to unusual ones and again we can prescribe the remedies according to which states of mind are most obvious.

Children's personalities can change a lot. There are plenty of challenging experiences throughout childhood and adolescence so if we are a parent and we want to help our children by using the remedies, our first priority is to keep the lines of communication open with our children. If we cannot understand and accept them for who they are and allow them to grow as nature intended they will naturally turn away from us and we will be unable to help them. However if they grow in a loving, encouraging and supportive environment where the parents are open, loving and communicative to each other and to their children then there is great hope for the children to become similarly well adjusted adults. Talking openly about our thoughts and feelings in relation to the Bach remedies can be a great way of discovering more about our own good qualities and areas that need improvement. Normally we might find this quite challenging but the remedies can help to promote a safer environment and provide an emotional 'camouflage' to help us feel more comfortable and less directly challenged when talking about our feelings.

The Bach Rescue Remedy and Rescue Remedy Cream are very useful to have around when children are growing up, they can be really useful for any kind of physical injury like falls, cuts and bruises and any sort of mental and emotional upset, they can quickly calm fears and shocks and generally help to soothe upset children and wound up parents!

Here is a list of the 38 remedies with brief indications; following this is a more detailed list of remedy profiles. You could use the following brief list to help you identify maybe eight or ten possible remedies then consult the detailed remedy descriptions before making your final choices. For more information on the remedies try reading *Bach Flower Remedies for Beginners* by David Vennells, published by Llewellyn.

Agrimony - mental torture behind a cheerful face

Aspen - fear of unknown things

Beech - intolerance

Centaury - the inability to say 'no'

Cerato - lack of trust in one's own decisions

Cherry Plum - fear of the mind giving way

Chestnut Bud - failure to learn from mistakes

Chicory - selfish, possessive love

Clematis - dreaming of the future, not in the present

Crab Apple - the cleansing remedy, also for self-hatred

Elm - overwhelmed by responsibility

Gentian - discouragement after a setback

Gorse - hopelessness and despair

Heather - self-centredness and self-concern

Holly - hatred, envy and jealousy

Honeysuckle - living in the past

Hornbeam - procrastination, tiredness at the thought of doing something

Impatiens - impatience

Larch - lack of confidence

Mimulus - fear of known things

Mustard - deep gloom for no reason

Oak - steady but sometimes slow person who may go past the point of exhaustion

Olive - exhaustion following mental or physical effort

Pine - guilt

Red Chestnut - over-concern for the welfare of loved ones

Rock Rose - terror and fright

Rock Water - self-denial, rigidity and self-repression

Scleranthus - inability to choose between alternatives

Star of Bethlehem - shock

Sweet Chestnut - Extreme mental anguish, when everything has been tried

Vervain - over-enthusiasm

Vine - dominance and inflexibility

Walnut - protection from change and unwanted influences

Water Violet - pride and aloofness

White Chestnut - unwanted thoughts and mental arguments

Wild Oat - uncertainty over one's direction in life

Wild Rose - drifting, resignation, apathy

Willow - self-pity and resentment

DETAILED REMEDY PROFILES

AGRIMONY

KEY WORDS: Hidden worries, outwardly cheerful

The Agrimony type hides their problems behind humour or fake cheerfulness, they find it difficult to talk openly about their problems, preferring to keep things bottled up inside. They often feel most at peace when they are on their own or with those they really trust, then they can let the mask of cheerfulness drop and finally express openly what is on their mind. It can take a long time for the Agrimony type to accept and trust another person, they tend to keep people emotionally at arm's length.

They also find it difficult to deal with other people's problems, especially if they are deep emotional ones. They may try to change the subject if they feel uncomfortable and try to pass things off lightly, often saying things like 'don't worry I'm sure everything will be OK' or 'well, that's life'. For them this is a way of avoiding their own inner worries and the prospect of having to face them or talk openly about them. They are often afraid of showing deep emotion in front of others and will present the 'stiff upper lip'.

ASPEN

KEY WORDS: Nervous, vague unspecific worries or fears

The Aspen person can be quite shy and quiet, their main personality trait is nervousness. Their physical actions are often quick, unsure and 'shaky'. The Aspen tree is sometimes called the 'trembling tree' and this is a good indication of the Aspen personality type. They are nervous and often lack confidence in themselves and in extreme cases their nervousness can lead to exhaustion and subsequent illness. There is a general sense of worry about these people. They may not necessarily be worried or frightened about something specific but just generally apprehensive. They can be quite superstitious and tend to dwell on negative things. They tend to think that bad things will come their way, nothing specific, they just generally feel that being alive is worrying and the future foreboding.

BEECH

Key Words: Critical, lacking tolerance and empathy

These people do not suffer fools easily! They have high standards and if others don't match up to these they are often looked down upon for falling short of their expectations. Parents who are severe Beech types may be quite strict and can pass these traits on to their children or the children can often feel inadequate and unworthy if they feel they do not meet their parents' high standards.

They generally have a lack of empathy towards others and find it difficult to understand another person's point of view. Again in the extreme case they feel that their own point of view is always correct. They are often traditionalists and find it difficult to understand why anyone would want to live their life in an unusual way; consequently they are often shocked when they hear about such people. Perhaps it threatens their sense of control and the fact that they feel more secure when things are 'in place'.

CENTAURY

KEY WORDS: Weak, easily influenced, overly willing servant

The Centaury person is generally not a leader; in fact often they are just the opposite. They like to be part of a team or following orders rather than giving them. They dislike responsibility and prefer to take a back seat and let others take decisions and then follow in their footsteps. They are often very kind, gentle and quiet people and do not like to rock the boat or cause any trouble for others and they do not like to draw attention to themselves. They are very willing helpers and they can often be found working in the 'caring' professions like nursing. They would certainly never go out of their way to hurt others and if someone were to hurt them they would tend to accept it without wanting revenge or feeling anger. They are more likely to cry quietly than get angry.

Others often treat the extreme Centaury quite badly, they can be easily taken advantage of or 'used'. They find it difficult to speak up and don't feel that they deserve respect from others, consequently others find it difficult to treat them with respect. They find it difficult to say 'No' and usually say yes to any request for help or command even if they really do not want to. This serves to leave them feeling even more weak and powerless. Many Centaury types develop a suppressed hatred of power or overt strength and often they have been bullied or abused at some point in their lives.

CERATO

KEY WORDS: Indecision, asking the advice and opinions of others

Cerato is one of the remedies for indecision. Cerato types find it difficult to have confidence in their own judgement. They are prone to be easily influenced by others. They find it difficult to take the lead in matters and have far more confidence in the decision-making abilities of anyone but themselves. They will tend to seek the advice of others rather than make their own mind up. They will often ask for suggestions and say things like, 'what do you think I should do?' or 'what would you do?' This constant habit of seeking others' advice does not actually help them and in fact causes them more confusion. When they finally make a decision they will continue to question it, often changing their minds several times before they finally decide one way or another. Even after a final decision is made and a course of action becomes irreversible they will continue to wonder how things might have been if they had done things differently.

CHERRY PLUM

KEY WORDS: Fear of insanity, of the mind giving way

The Cherry Plum type is likely to be very mentally or emotionally strained. They may feel that they cannot cope any more and be frightened that their mind might soon give way. This remedy is also indicated when there is fear of the impulse to do harm to oneself or to another. There may be a lack of rationality and they may often feel commanded by their own thoughts and impulses. These feelings might be bottled up for fear that others might think that they are losing their mind, this only makes things worse and puts more internal pressure on them. This remedy is also helpful after long periods of stress or strain, for example during a long illness after a period of heavy work or study or at any time when the patient feels they have reached their inner limits.

CHESTNUT BUD

KEY WORDS: Always repeating the same mistake, not learning from experience

Chestnut Bud is an ideal remedy for those who are trapped in a cycle of repetitive behaviour. They find it hard to learn from experience and tend to make the same mistake many times before they finally realise that another course of action might be better. This can be quite a damaging state of mind especially if it results in, for example, a series of damaging relationships all with the same destructive qualities.

Sometimes these people do not realise that they are making the same mistake again. They can be quite naïve and live in a semi-fantasy world where reality is not always welcome. They may tend to reject or avoid the advice of others especially if it threatens their own view on life. Often they are aware that they are making the same mistake again but actually cannot help themselves, even if they know that there is a strong chance that they will be hurt or that they will hurt someone else. For the Chestnut Bud type the cycle of negative repetitive behaviour can almost be an addiction.

CHICORY

KEY WORDS: Over protective, mothering/smothering

Chicory people care too much! They are liable to be overbearing and find it difficult to give their loved ones the space to breath. They are over protective and often instil in their children the belief that the world is a dangerous place and that they need protection. They gain a great deal of satisfaction from caring for others, indeed they strongly identify themselves with this role to the extent that if they have no one to care for they may feel lost and worthless.

They may have difficulty in letting go of others and experience great distress when those they care for are in any kind of danger. They can dread the future if they know at some point that those they care for will have to go their own way. For example the Chicory parent will not look forward to their children leaving home, especially if they are moving far away. As this time approaches they will become more and more clingy and controlling and this often has the effect of making the children want to mover sooner or further away.

CLEMATIS

KEY WORDS: Dreamy, sleepy, forgetful, always thinking about the future

Clematis people can appear to be living in a little world of their own. A fantasy world where everything is as it should be, no problems, no hassles, no worries. They like to take things slowly and at their own pace and do not like to pressured into quick decisions as they easily get confused and cannot think clearly, especially under stress. They are often absent-minded, forgetting appointments, mislaying keys, etc. Many Clematis folk have a poor sense of direction and although they are often creative and sensitive they are not naturally practical and not very reliable in a crisis.

Their dreamy state of mind is usually dwelling on happy fantasies of how they would like things to be in the future. Although the Clematis likes to have something to look forward to and longs for happier times they do not do much to bring these events about. They tend to lack interest in the present, prefer to avoid tough situations and do not like talking about subjects that challenge their dreamy attitude. Their fantasy world feels safer than the world outside and is within their control. They do not like 'real' life and prefer their own inner world. Unfortunately they miss out on so much in life because of this. They often lose the track of a conversation, forget what they were saying, and easily become bored or distracted and therefore sometimes lack the ability to concentrate.

CRAB APPLE

KEY WORDS: *Feeling dirty and unclean*

This is the cleansing remedy for those who feel they are not clean in some way, as if they are 'infected' or feel sullied or used. This feeling may follow a physical cause like disease, or being affected by some kind of pollution or toxic substance. The sufferer still feels that they are not clean, even after vigorous washing. These feelings may also arise after spending time with another person who you mistrust or in an extreme case 'makes your flesh creep'. Perhaps they have been in your car and even after a few days you can still sense their presence and the space feels unclean or polluted in some way. Crab Apple people easily feel contaminated and are often over cautious about dirt, germs and infections.

ELM

KEY WORDS: *Overwhelmed by responsibility*

Elm people are often very capable people usually occupying positions of authority or responsibility. They enjoy a challenge and the feeling that they are doing something useful and successful. However from time to time they may feel the pressure of responsibility is overwhelming; this can become so great that they feel they cannot go on. This is often only a temporary period of self-doubt and they usually pull through. Although there is a danger that if they experience some additional problems during one of these periods they may believe that their confidence and ability to deal with pressure will never return. Consequently they may make decisions to change jobs or finish relationships that they later regret when again they are feeling stronger and more able to cope.

GENTIAN

KEY WORDS: Despondency, despair, discouragement

Gentian is the remedy for those people who give up easily when they experience any difficulty or set back in their affairs. They are inclined to feel that there is no point in going on and they stop trying or making an effort to achieve. They often have good intentions at the start of a project and they are never short of good ideas but they do not have much staying power and become easily discouraged when things don't go according to plan or there is a series of minor set backs. Generally Gentian is a good remedy for anyone who suffers any kind of set back like failing an exam, missing out on a promotion or new job, relationship problems, etc.

GORSE

KEY WORDS: Deep despondency and despair

Gorse is indicated whenever someone is so low that it seems nothing will comfort them or lift them out of their despondency. Gorse differs from

Gentian in that people in the latter category will tend to 'pick up' after a short time of self doubt; their condition is not so severe. The Gorse type, if left to their own devices, will tend to get worse and even more withdrawn. They often feel that there is no hope for them and that they have reached the end of the line. The atmosphere that surrounds the Gorse person is very heavy, there is a definite sense that there is no hope even trying and that the battle was lost long ago. When they are ill they do not try to get better or think positively, they give in to whatever difficulty they are experiencing and sometimes do not expect to get well at all. If they do try some form of treatment they do not expect it to work. They can be quite difficult to care for as the carer receives little gratitude and often just complaints and comments like, 'it's not worth it' or 'what's the point?'.

HEATHER

KEY WORDS: Need to talk, not good listeners

The Heather type likes to be listened to. They like the sound of their own voice and the more people that hear it the better! They especially like to talk about their worries, problems and ailments or anything about themselves their family and friends. They will try to control the conversation and constantly bring it back to their own problems. They can be quite tiring and draining people almost like energetic vampires! They are physical people and like to express themselves with arm gestures and loud exclamations. They will often touch others in conversation to keep their attention and to express an emotion. They are generally not good listeners and easily get bored and frustrated with other people's conversation, especially if it about something that doesn't involve them or on a subject about which they know little. They tend to jump-in before the other person has finished what they were saying and use some small point of their conversation as an excuse for them to start talking again.

HOLLY

KEY WORDS: *Strong negative emotions like envy, suspicion, and revenge*

Holly is the remedy for combating heavy negativity that takes the form of hatred, envy, rage, etc. The Holly state can arise when someone has been emotionally hurt, they may find it difficult to think rationally and have repetitive negative thoughts and feelings towards another. Often it can be related to things that have happened in the past, like difficult childhood experiences which have not been fully accepted. Jealousy is another common Holly emotion; the sufferer may feel very unhappy that another person is experiencing good things. It is quite an immature state of mind, although we all have it sometimes! It is a common remedy for children learning the lessons of growing up.

HONEYSUCKLE

KEY WORDS: *Dreamy, nostalgic, dwelling on the past*

Honeysuckle types tend to spend much time thinking about how things used to be; the good old days! They look at the past as being much better than the present even if in reality things were in fact harder. They are escapists like the Clematis types and often appear dreamy and 'not all there'. Many older people develop these mental and emotional habits, especially if they are physically and mentally inactive or unhappy in their old age. They dwell on the past, on happier times and relive memories over and over in their minds. They might be surrounded by old photographs perhaps of their children and this serves to keep them locked in to the past. They have little interest in the present; they can become forgetful and lose concentration easily. In fact any one who is experiencing difficulties of any sort may find themselves thinking back to happier times when life was easier and they were surrounded by good things.

HORNBEAM
KEY WORDS: Lack of enthusiasm, weariness
When the thought of having to do something you do not want to do makes you feel tired and lacking strength or energy then Hornbeam is indicated. It is the remedy for that 'Monday morning' feeling when you would prefer to go back to bed rather than face another week at work!

It can be used in many situations like having to visit someone you are obliged to see now and again, having to go to a party or other event when you would prefer to stay at home, having to do mundane or menial tasks that you would prefer someone else to do. Whenever we are faced with a situation that we would prefer to avoid and the thought of having to go through with it leaves us feeling tired and listless then Hornbeam can help. Hornbeam is not the remedy for exhaustion or fatigue due to illness or overwork, Olive would suit these symptoms.

IMPATIENS
KEY WORDS: Impatience, irritation, frustration
Impatiens is the remedy for those people who are quick in thought and deed. They do not suffer fools gladly and become easily irritated when others are doing things too slowly or holding them back or making them wait in some way. They easily lose their temper and are prone to speak critically. They often prefer to work on their own without the interference of others and they like to get things done quickly and efficiently.

Impatiens types do not like queuing, sitting in traffic or waiting for service, they think that everyone else should be as efficient and swift as they are. They are often quick learners and intelligent although sometimes they get uptight if they cannot get their head round a problem.

LARCH

KEY WORDS: Lack of confidence

This remedy is helpful for those people who lack confidence in their own ability to succeed in any situation. Although in fact they are usually very capable people they lack the self-belief to make the most of these abilities; because of this they may miss out on many opportunities in life. They tend to stand back and allow others, often less capable than themselves, to move ahead of them in life and then they look at these people moving on and think, 'I could have done that'. Consequently they can become quite lonely and resentful later in life, although these states of mind should be treated with different remedies. This remedy can also be used for temporary loss of confidence when we have, for example, failed an exam, crashed our car or felt any kind of rejection.

MIMULUS

KEY WORDS: Fear of known things

Mimulus is for the shy, quiet types who tend to avoid confrontation and like to lead a peaceful life. They are quite sensitive people who readily take an interest in others' problems as long as they are not too difficult or challenging. They do not have a strong constitution and easily become nervous or worried sometimes about the smallest things. They are sometimes so shy that they avoid talking to others whenever possible. They do not like crowds and social gatherings and especially dislike loud, confident, aggressive or boastful people. They are very polite and also find it difficult to say no and consequently can be easily intimidated and taken advantage of.

They may blush or stammer during conversation and sometimes especially in the presence of the opposite sex or people they do not know well. Although they may be quite romantic they rarely have the confidence to go and talk to someone they might find attractive. They are very self-conscious and easily embarrassed and do not like to draw attention to themselves and the thought of having to speak to a crowd of people would leave them feeling sick with fear. This also the remedy for any kind of specific or known fear, for example fear of public speaking, the dark, spiders, heights, travelling, poverty, loneliness, illness, death, etc.

MUSTARD

KEY WORDS: Depression that descends and lifts quickly

Mustard is one of the remedies for depression, mainly the depressive state of mind that descends quickly like a heavy cloud over the sufferer. When in the middle of this depression it seems that it might last a long time and there is a feeling that there is no light at the end of the tunnel. Sometimes they may have no strong feelings, good or bad, about anything, just a kind of mental and emotional dullness and lack of joy. This state of mind can lift as quickly and mysteriously as it came although often it can last for weeks and sometimes months, it may descend and lift in unpredictable cycles.

It can almost seem that the sufferer is two people - the normal one and the one that appears during the periods of depression. Although a series of stressful events can spark off a period of Mustard depression there is generally no specific cause. They may not be able to actually find a reason why they feel so deeply unhappy, it just seems as if unhappiness has arisen from within and they cannot do anything but sit in it until it naturally lifts.

OAK

KEY WORDS: Strong, steady, reliable type

This remedy is for those people who are generally steady and reliable. They are regarded as someone who will never let the side down and can always be relied upon to be there when they are needed. People often turn to them in times of trouble and they appear never to be shaken or stirred by stressful events.

They tend to take life at their own pace and are not easily influenced by changing fashions and 'fads'. Sometimes they do not like change and they might stay in the same house, job and relationship for years. Consequently they may appear to be boring to others and lack creativity and spontaneity. They may feel a strong sense of duty and responsibility to others so much so that they might take on too much work or agree to help others even when they actually need to rest themselves.

They generally have great stamina and staying power. They tend never to give up and when they have set themselves a goal they will keep on trying at a steady almost relentless pace until they achieve what they set out to do. They do not give in when the going gets tough and they are carry on even in the face of great adversity. When ill they will struggle on with their duties and are rarely known to take time off work or complain that they are being worked too hard.

OLIVE

KEY WORDS: Physical and mental exhaustion

Olive is the remedy for extreme fatigue. The sufferer feels so tired and run down that they cannot go on and wish to give up. They feel that their energy and strength have all but gone and that they have nothing in reserve. Olive can be used by anyone who feels tired and depleted after dealing with any stressful event. This state of exhaustion may follow a long period of illness where the sufferer has had to put up with much physical and mental pain or stress. If it seems that things are not going to improve then the thought of facing the future makes them feel even weaker.

Olive is not a 'type' remedy although some people are more prone to giving away their time and energy to others in an unskilful way that often leaves them feeling they have nothing left to give. So this remedy is very helpful for carers who feel they have given everything to the person they are looking after and all their energy is sapped, sometimes they may even feel drained of love and concern for the other, and this indicates other remedies as well.

PINE

KEY WORDS: Guilt, self blame

Pine is the remedy for those people who are always blaming themselves, sometimes for things that are obviously not their fault. They tend to be quite hard on themselves and their thought patterns often take on a quality of self-punishment. They often do not feel 'good enough' and may feel that a sense of guilt is a good thing. These people often come from strict backgrounds, they may have been taught to believe from an early age that talking pleasure in the good things in life is bad.

They may find it difficult to relax and their strong standards and opinions about what is wrong or sinful may surface as revulsion towards others. They may feel emotions and desires but try to ignore them or keep them within. If they do allow their minds to wander on to such thoughts they may feel guilty. Pine types also tend to apologise too much.

RED CHESTNUT

KEY WORDS: *Fear for the welfare of others*

The Red Chestnut remedy is ideal for people who feel fear or great concern for the welfare of others. In the extreme case this is not a healthy compassionate concern but more a selfish feeling based on the fact that the Red Chestnut type only feels at peace when those they love are at not risk from anything. They can be very overprotective parents always saying, 'be careful' or 'don't run so fast you might fall'. When their children are playing they often check on them every few minutes to see if they are safe. They may run through in their mind all the things that might happen to their child if they are not there to protect and guide them. Even when their children are grown up they may always want to know that they are safe and well. It can also be used as a temporary remedy for anyone who is overly concerned about the welfare of another.

ROCK ROSE

KEY WORDS: *Extreme fear, terror*

Rock Rose is not a type remedy but is used in the occasional situations of extreme fear. The fear so grips the sufferer that they are almost paralysed and sometimes cannot even talk about what has happened or what they are presently afraid of. This is definitely not nervousness or fear like the Mimulus or Aspen state. This is much more severe and deep-seated.

This remedy can be very helpful after a nightmare when we have been gripped by terror or the belief that our life might be in danger. Also children who awake from frightening dreams find relief from using Rock

Rose. Any real life situation that creates terror can call for this remedy, for example, after a serious car crash, being attacked, taking a fall, etc. Also the fear of these things happening can also be treated with Rock Rose if the feelings of fear are extreme, if not then Mimulus is the right remedy to choose. For example, some people are extremely afraid of heights, flying, undergoing surgery, etc.

ROCK WATER
KEY WORDS: Strict, high almost severe standards
The people that fit the Rock Water type are very hard on themselves. Whatever their vocation or interests in life they take them very seriously, almost too seriously. They can almost be fanatical about whatever they are interested in. If they like sports or outdoor pursuits they will set themselves excessively hard targets or goals and often push themselves too far in trying to achieve them. They like to have a set routine that they stick to, even if it is causing them pain or distress. They do not like to feel that they are weak or incapable and do not like others to think this either, so again they will push themselves sometimes beyond their limits so as not to appear to fail.

Their high and harsh standards also manifest as mental and emotional rigidity, they may find it difficult to express their emotions and prefer to keep them in or go and work them out at the gym! They may live a military-style life and might expect others to fall in line. They like to run a tight ship and if they are the head of the family they find it difficult to tolerate laziness or shoddiness in themselves or others, although they tend not to openly criticise or 'convert' others but try to lead by example. When they have spare time they prefer to do something 'useful'.

SCLERANTHUS

KEY WORDS: Quiet indecision, always changing their mind

Scleranthus like Cerato is the remedy for indecision. However these personality types are quite different. Whilst Ceratos are always being swayed by the opinions of others, the Scleranthus type keeps their worries and concerns to themselves. They may have a problem or have to make a decision but rather than ask for help they will mull things over in their own mind. Others may not even realise that they have a problem.

This indecision is not confined to major issues as the Scleranthus type has difficulty making any kind of decision like what clothes to wear, what to eat, whether to phone or write to someone. Even after a decision is made doubt remains and they are prone to changing their minds several times before making their final decision. They can be so indecisive that they become confused; their mind spins with ideas and possibilities. They tend to think about things too much and the consequences of their actions or potential actions. Because they keep their ideas to themselves this adds to their problems and prevents them from benefiting from the wisdom and experience of others.

STAR OF BETHLEHEM

KEY WORDS: Shock

This remedy is excellent for treating people who have experienced any kind of severe shock, recent or from many years before. The shock might be a serious accident, the death of a loved one, a burglary or other criminal act, very bad news, a horrific or appalling sight etc. Sometimes it might not be an obvious or sudden shock, for example a long-term problem like financial worries or illness may leave the sufferer looking back on what has happened to them and feel shocked at how their life has changed.

People who need Star of Bethlehem may seem bewildered, lost and in a kind of daze when they talk about their problems. They might say that they feel they have been caught up in a whirlwind of problems and that their feet have not touched the ground or they might say, 'I can't believe what has happened to me'. There is a sense of disbelief of being knocked sideways and not feeling 'all here' as a result. In severe emergency cases the sufferer may be shaking, unable to talk or lose consciousness.

SWEET CHESTNUT

KEY WORDS: Severe mental distress, anguish

Sweet Chestnut is the remedy for extreme mental and emotional anguish. When this remedy is indicated the sufferer is usually so distraught that they cannot be consoled or comforted. They are in a state of psychological distress; there is a sense of great despair and loss of hope. They feel that no solution to their problems can be found, as if there is no light at the end of the tunnel and that all that the future holds is more suffering. They may actually wish to die but tend to believe that even death would not release them from their great distress. These feelings may accompany any major life problem like the loss of a loved one, severe financial problems, long term illness or anything that results in severe mental turmoil.

VERVAIN

KEY WORDS: Over enthusiastic, physical and mental strain

Vervain folk are very conscientious and hard working. They have high ideals and standards and it is often their mission in life to help others see that their ways are best! They can be quite evangelical and try to convert others to their way of thinking. They do this not for the sense of power or control but because they have genuinely good intentions and wish to help others. Their boundless enthusiasm might often be for environmental, educational, political or spiritual issues or for some other good cause and whenever they have a chance to talk to someone about these they will do their best to interest others in these worthy causes. They like to show others the way!

They often make good salesmen and women and their enthusiasm can be infectious and lead them to be successful in whatever field they choose. However they can be prone to working or pushing themselves too far and this can lead to physical and mental strain and tension. They can become frustrated if they feel their work is not progressing well or if problems and difficulties arise. They tend to be quick thinking and active people, full of good ideas and good intentions.

VINE

KEY WORDS: Leadership, powerful and controlling attitude

Vine is the remedy for those people who are the natural leaders in society. They are attracted to roles in life where they can lead and influence others. In the extreme negative state they enjoy power or authority and exercise control in a manipulative and self-centred manner. Sometimes their wish for power, dominance and control is so great that they will do anything to reach a position of authority and once there do anything to keep it. The classic extreme vine type is the military dictator who is feared by his subjects and servants.

The positive Vine type is an excellent leader and a great example to others. The typical Vine type might have a responsible job where they are in charge of a large department or company, often with many people under their influence. If they are a benevolent and kind boss people will love and look up to them. If they are a 'tin-pot' dictator they often end up feeling lonely and separate from their employees.

WALNUT

KEY WORDS: *Easily influenced by others*

Walnut is the remedy for protection. It is not generally seen as a type remedy but some people will be more likely to use this remedy than others. The people that will most benefit from Walnut are those who are easily influenced by others. We all experience a certain amount of nervousness or vulnerability at times of change or upheaval and these are the indications for Walnut. Examples of when Walnut might be appropriate are when moving house, emigrating, changing jobs, gaining promotion, getting married, having your first child, beginning a new relationship. Basically any major change to your routine that leaves you feeling a little disorientated and 'out of sorts'. It can also help us cut mental and emotional ties with the past that might be holding us back and preventing us giving our full energy to new situations and new relationships.

WATER VIOLET

KEY WORDS: *Proud, aloof, quiet*

Water Violet types can be seen by others as being very proud and sometimes superior. They may not see themselves as proud but they often do feel superior to others. They can look down on those around them, see them as being coarse or ignorant and feel that they are on a higher mental or spiritual level than others. This can lead to a lonely existence, as they feel unable to open up and talk to others about their problems unless they feel the other person is on the same wavelength.

They are often quiet and thoughtful people and do not like large crowds, noisy rooms, or energetic parties. They prefer their own company or that of a few well-known and trusted friends. Their natural disposition is generally positive and confident and like the plant itself they often stand proud and erect. Their physical movement is often graceful and elegant and they are rarely rushed or erratic.

WHITE CHESTNUT

KEY WORDS: Unwanted disturbing thoughts

The White Chestnut remedy is useful when a person is unable to prevent unwanted and often distressing thoughts and emotions arising in the mind. There is a lack of mental peace and the sufferer is plagued by constant and often unfounded worries or they just cannot switch off. Sometimes this condition may be more noticeable at night or when resting from daily activity, when there are fewer external distractions to occupy the mind. As a result of this condition many people become tired and worn out as they find it difficult to sleep, they may also wake up frequently and their mind automatically returns to the worrying thoughts. Also the amount of mental energy they use up and the constant stress of the agitated mind can leave them feeling confused and worn out. Often the White Chestnut person will appear to be thinking about something else even whilst in conversation, as if their mind is elsewhere. There might not necessarily be an obvious cause for the persistent thoughts; the mind is just in the habit of thinking rather than relaxing and being.

WILD OAT

KEY WORDS: Looking for direction or purpose

The Wild Oat person can often seem listless, bored and without energy.

This is due to their lack of direction or purpose in life. Often they have experienced much and may have had many jobs, partners, change of addresses but it is as if they are still searching for something. They may become tired, disillusioned and aimless because of their searching. It is also a mental searching and they often spend time wondering about what they should be doing with their lives but never come up with anything that really grabs them. If they do find something that they think might be right for them they will often try it for a short time then change their minds and go searching again.

They can be quite immature people and appear not to have grown up, a sort of adolescent adult. They may not actually want to take responsibility for their lives and instead prefer to 'play around' and loaf, rather than find a useful occupation or career. This might show in their behaviour and the way they treat others.

WILD ROSE

KEY WORDS: Apathy, laziness

The Wild Rose type has little interest in anything. They are lazy and prefer to do nothing rather than try to change things for the better. They are apathetic and lack interest in the welfare of others and even themselves. The extreme Wild Rose type has given up caring about anything, often teenagers go through a Wild Rose phase. They often feel heavy and tired, lacking energy and vitality. They are not creative or spontaneous and prefer to keep away from people who disturb their wish for a quiet and easy life.

Often they may end up without a job or with one that is very undemanding. They lack imagination and energy, they have no ambition to move on or better themselves but prefer to accept things as they are and drift along through life applying as little effort as possible. They might say things like, 'that's life', 'that's just the way things are', 'don't rock the boat'.

WILLOW

KEY WORDS: Introspective, self-obsessed

The Willow type of person reacts to difficulties and problems by becoming quiet, withdrawn and introspective. They can be quite melancholic and enjoy wallowing in their own problems. This can bring others down and just being in the presence of a severe Willow type can leave you feeling low and heavy. They also tend to sap the energy of others in a similar way to the Heather type. Although these types are similar in that they are both self-obsessed they are opposites in the way that they try to gain the attention of others, the Heather being openly talkative and the Willow more quiet and sulky.

The Willow will dwell on their own problems and past misfortune, the sadness they feel is strangely comforting and there is a subtle sense of self-righteousness in their suffering. They may feel resentful towards others or towards life, wondering why they have been so unfortunate. There is a definite 'why me?' attitude and this is accentuated if others close to them are more fortunate or successful in life. They can become trapped in this cycle of self-pity, grumbling and moaning whenever they have an opportunity.

7
HOMEOPATHY

Homeopathy is one of the most well known forms of modern complementary therapy. The remedies are widely available, the internet is full of information about homeopathy, many doctors use it alongside conventional medicine and there is a long list of famous people who are happy to be known to use it, including many of the European Royal Families who have been using it since Victorian times. The popularity of homeopathy is based on its effectiveness as a complete system of natural healing. There are many accounts of homeopathy being effective for all kinds of illnesses and there is also a growing body of medical evidence to support such claims.

Homeopathy is the second most widely used system of medicine in the world. Its growth in popularity in the US has been around 25 to 50 percent a year throughout the last decade, this success is fueled by several factors:

Homeopathy is extremely effective; when the correct remedy is taken, results can be rapid, complete and permanent.

Homeopathy is completely safe, even babies and pregnant women can use it.

Homeopathy works without the danger of side effects. Homeopathic remedies can also be taken alongside other medication without producing unwanted side effects.

Homeopathy is natural; the remedies are normally based on natural ingredients.

Homeopathy works in harmony with your immune system, unlike some conventional medicines which suppress the immune system.

Homeopathic remedies are not addictive - once relief is felt, you should stop taking them. If no relief is felt, you are probably taking the wrong homeopathic remedy.

Homeopathy tries to address the cause, not the symptoms; this often means that symptoms do not recur.

Homeopathy is based on treating like with like. The same principle is widespread in mainstream medicine, the most notable examples being antidotes and vaccines. However homeopathy takes this idea a step further. If the symptoms of an illness are *similar* to the symptoms from a tarantula's bite, then tarantula venom would be the homeopathic remedy. The theory that like can be treated with like can be traced back as far as Hypocrites, but it wasn't until the work of Samuel Hahnemann (1755-1843) that the theory developed into a usable practice.

Hahnemann's 'provings' consisted of giving doses of various substances to both himself and his healthy volunteers, and noting the effects in detail. For safety reasons, the substances taken were very dilute, and it is here that Hahnemann chanced upon one of the more puzzling aspects of homeopathy. The more dilute a homeopathic medicine is, the more effective it is in treating illness.

Hahnemann's work was continued by James Tyler Kent in 1878. Kent's interest in homoeopathic medicine was prompted by his wife's serious illness, which failed to respond to any other form of medicine available at the time. Kent's position as Professor of Anatomy (at the American Medical College, St Louis) placed him perfectly to observe the effects of substances in precise detail. Kent's research into homeopathy became his life's work, and he conducted provings on some 650 materials, observing over 64,000 symptoms. Even today, Kent's is still the most widely used repertory in homeopathy.

Classical homeopathy may seem unusual to those used to conventional medicine, where one medicine is taken for a skin complaint, another for a headache, and yet another for sleeplessness. A common cold, for example, is one virus which produces a myriad of effects. Different people with a cold caused by the same virus may exhibit different symptoms. It is for this reason that each case should be assessed by close and careful analysis of all the relevant symptoms. The Similium is the single substance which if given to a healthy person would produce exactly the same symptoms as exhibited by the patient.

So broadly speaking homeopathic remedies are a system of medicine based on three principles:

Like cures like: For example, if the symptoms of your cold are similar to poisoning by mercury, then mercury would be your homeopathic remedy. But obviously in a very dilute and safe dose.

Minimal dose: The remedy is taken in an extremely dilute form, normally one part of the remedy to around 1,000,000,000,000 parts of water.

The single remedy: No matter how many symptoms are experienced, only one remedy is taken, and that remedy will be aimed at all those symptoms.

There are two main barriers to the effective use of homeopathy. Firstly prescribing the right homeopathic remedy takes a little more time and patience than conventional medicine. Exactly the right remedy needs to be taken for your symptoms. There is no such thing as a standard homeopathic headache remedy. The remedy you take has to be matched to your particular headache - where it occurs, what brings it on, what type of pain it is, what aggravates it, what makes it feel worse, your state of mind and what other symptoms you experience. Secondly the sheer range of remedies in use can cause practical problems for an average sized pharmacy.

However there are about thirty remedies which are very useful and easily available and simple to prescribe. If you want to look in to the possibility of searching through the full remedies to find one that is suitable for you it is better to speak to a qualified homeopath or try one of the free on-line diagnostic websites like www.abchomeopathy.com. or www. homeopath.com.

Not all homeopaths agree on dosage and potency, and the potency to be taken depends on both the sensitivity of the patient and the remedy being taken. But as a general rule, chronic illnesses (i.e. those that last for a long time) should be treated with high numbers i.e. 30C-200C and acute illnesses with low numbers i.e 6C.

Low numbers like 6C indicate a less dilute remedy, but work more effectively on the physical level for short illnesses like a virus:cold and physical injuries like sprains, burns, insect bites etc.

High numbers like 30-200C are highly diluted, more potent or subtle and work more effectively on the mental, emotional and spiritual levels. Healing on these levels is often the key to healing or alleviating long term illness.

However, there are exceptions, particularly where an accident started off the symptoms and you might give the body a kick start with a high potency dose such as Arnica 200C first and then follow with a lower potency remedy. Low numbers are used more frequently than high numbers. Another general rule is that high potency homeopathic medicine should only be taken when you know it is the right remedy, so start off with a low potency remedy, and then increase the potency if improvement is felt, though incomplete.

Homeopathic medicine should be taken on a clean pallet. While on a course of homeopathic treatment, you should avoid strong flavours such as mint (including toothpaste), coffee or camphor. The remedies are normally taken as pills which are placed under the tongue. Generally two tablets every two hours for the first six doses, and then four times daily for up to five days. For some complaints remedies are taken as an ointment, for example, arnica cream applied directly to bruising. If you are taking the remedy in pill form, you should avoid contact with the skin. Just drop the pills into the lid and put them directly into the mouth. Once relief from the symptoms is felt, stop taking the homeopathic medicine. Only take it again if exactly the same symptoms come back.

The basic aim of homeopathic prescribing is to find the one remedy which best matches all your symptoms. As homeopathy relies on prescribing remedies to your precise combination of symptoms, all your symptoms should be included in the process. Most of us have a few niggles that have been with us so long we don't even notice them anymore, these all need your full attention. You should also include things which you might not even class as symptoms, such as a persistent itch behind your ear.

Aside from the obvious nature of your complaint things to notice include:

- State of mind including fears, anxieties, attitudes, etc.
- What makes a particular symptom feel worse or better?

- Where exactly is each problem located?
- When did symptoms first occur, and what brought them on?
- Your sleep pattern.
- Sensitivity, i.e. light, cold, heat, drafts, touch, criticism, etc.

The most important thing when attempting to diagnose and treat illnesses at home is to know when to stop. If symptoms persist, go and see your doctor; even if you feel your symptoms seem unworthy of professional help. Long term chronic illnesses are deeper rooted than short term acute illnesses, and are consequently more difficult to treat successfully at home; normally guidance from a homeopath should be sought. Short term illnesses can be treated much more successfully at home.

How homeopathy actually works remains a mystery. Chemists have concluded that in the very high homeopathic potencies there is actually none of the original substance left. Theories explaining homeopathy have been put forward resting on vibrations, life force energy, electromagnetism, or the memory of water. Perhaps these questions will be answered in the future, all that we can say for now is that there is definitely a homeopathic effect when the right remedy is taken and this has been verified by countless successful treatments and some medical research programmes.

Here is a list of some remedies that are suitable for self prescription and can be bought as either 6C or 30C potency at any health store. If you want to search through the thousands of other remedies available it is best to visit a qualified homeopath or try one of the free on-line databases where you can often also order the remedies.

Aconite

Symptoms: sweating, palpitations, pain, chills and fever, feelings of fear, anxiety, shock; symptoms begin suddenly, are acute or at an early stage and are triggered by exposure to cold, dry winds.

Uses: sore throats, earache, teething, coughs, colds, chest complaints, cystitis, eye inflammations, early stages of chickenpox, mumps or measles, bleeding in pregnancy, labour pains, anxiety, fear and shock.

Allium Cepa

Symptoms: streaming eyes and nose, discharge, catarrh, sneezing, headache, sore throats.

Uses: common colds, catarrhal headaches, runny nose, eye inflammation, sore throats, hay fever, tickly cough.

Apis mel

Symptoms: pain, swelling, burning or stinging sensation, red face and/or tongue, feelings of restlessness or fear; symptoms get worse with touch and heat and are better when outside.

Uses: bites and stings, hives, rashes, fever with dry skin, cystitis, headache, earache, sore throats, sore eyes, nappy rash, scarlet fever, irritability, tearfulness, fear of being alone.

Arnica

Symptoms: bruising, soreness, injury, shock, trauma, smelly breath, not wanting to be touched.

Uses: bruises, swelling, sprains and strains, shock, trauma, joint pain, bleeding gums, jet lag, cough with bruised feeling from coughing, broken veins, nosebleeds due to injury, abdominal and labour pains, bad breath, fearfulness and forgetfulness after injury. Do not apply to broken skin or open wounds.

Arsen Alb

Symptoms: sensitivity to cold, dry and cracked lips, burning pains, feelings of restlessness, fear and irritability, thirst, discharges; symptoms get better with heat and worse in cold or damp, after midnight and on waking.

Uses: acute colds and flu with burning nasal discharge, loose or dry cough, usually dry at night, dry and sore lips, fever and chills, burns, breathlessness, headache, indigestion, vomiting due to food poisoning, nausea, sore throat, headache, sleeplessness, diarrhoea.

Belladonna

Symptoms: sudden appearance and disappearance of symptoms, violent throbbing pain, dilated pupils, sweat, shock; symptoms worsened by movement and often worst around 3am and 3pm.

Uses: burning fever in children, throbbing headaches, swollen glands, intolerance to light, fever associated with chickenpox, measles, mumps or scarlet fever, sunstroke, teething and sore throats, earache, labour pains, convulsions, rage, delirium.

Bryonia

Symptoms: dry mouth and lips, sweat, bitter taste, sore pain, dark face and tongue, dizziness, irritability, slow onset; symptoms are worst around 9pm and after weather changes but better when lying still or on receiving firm pressure.

Uses: joint pain and swelling, broken bones with stitching pain, dry, painful cough, fever and flu with bitter taste, mastitis, measles and mumps with dislike of movement, diarrhoea, dizziness, eye inflammation, depression and a feeling of wanting to be left alone.

Calendula

Symptoms: wounds and cuts with pain out of proportion to injury.

Uses: cuts and open wounds, abscesses, burns, general tissue healing, perineal tears during birth or episiotomy; can be applied as an ointment and/or taken internally and can be alternated with arnica.

Cantharis

Symptoms: sudden, intense and spasmodic pain, constant desire to urinate, hot and scanty urine, severe thirst; symptoms worse before, during and after urination and after cold drinks.

Uses: cystitis, serious scalds or burns with blisters, burning sensation in throat, severe anxiety.

Causticum

Symptoms: affected by weather change especially chilly and dry weather, exhaustion, blisters, loss of appetite in pregnancy; symptoms worst in the evening.

Uses: serious burns (can be used on way to hospital), bedwetting, cystitis and stress incontinence, cramp in toes and feet, hacking coughs with phlegm that's difficult to cough up, hoarseness especially in the morning, painful joints eased by warmth, restless legs, poor concentration, tearfulness over minor matters.

Chamomilla

Symptoms: unbearable pain, feeling overemotional; symptoms get better after sweating.

Uses: teething, toothache, earache, colic, dry cough worst at night, labour pains, menstrual pains, vomiting from anger or excitement.

Coffea

Symptoms: overexcitement, oversensitivity, symptoms worse at night and in fresh air.

Uses: teething and toothache with shooting pain that's eased by cold drinks, labour pains with excitability and talkativeness, sleeplessness and vivid dreams.

Drosera

Symptoms: difficult breathing, hacking coughs; symptoms worst after midnight and when lying down or talking, but eased by pressure.

Uses: severe coughs, coughing fits, chest infections, coughs that develop after measles, sore throat, hoarseness.

Euphrasia

Symptoms: irritating discharge; symptoms worst in the morning.

Uses: eye inflammation and discharge, watery eyes, eyestrain especially from computer use, hay fever with sore eyes, mild measles with cold and eye problems, common cold with irritating nasal catarrh and watery eyes.

Gelsemium

Symptoms: exhaustion, heaviness, drowsiness, lack of thirst; symptoms are gradual and worse after physical exertion but better after sweating or urination.

Uses: fevers with shivering but no sweat, flu with aching muscles and heaviness, dizziness, measles with slow onset, no thirst, drowsiness, fever and chills, diarrhoea, labour pains, painful periods, anxiety during pregnancy, fear of specific things.

Hamamelis

Symptoms: acute minor bleeding, pain that feels worse when touched.

Uses: minor bleeding, burns, cuts, wounds and abrasions, nosebleeds, piles, varicose veins especially during and after pregnancy, swollen veins, bladder inflammation, heavy periods, tender and rheumatic joints.

Hepar sulph

Symptoms: dislike of cold, sensitivity to pain, desire for sour food, feeling impulsive, irritable and oversensitive; symptoms worst at night and after exposure to dry cold.

Uses: inflamed or festering cuts and wounds, sensitive irritated skin, boils and abscesses, eye inflammation, earache, toothache, barking coughs and croup, joint pain, swollen glands, mastitis and cracked nipples due to breastfeeding, athlete's foot.

Hypericum

Symptoms: nerve damage, intense pain, sensitivity to touch, shock.

Uses: nerve pain due to dental treatment, surgery, splinters, accidents or after forceps delivery; insect bites and stings, animal bites, back pain due to childbirth or injury, painful periods that are late and accompanied by headache.

Ignatia

Symptoms: contradictory symptoms, such as an empty feeling in stomach which isn't relieved by eating; grief, despair, disappointment, aggravated by stimulants such as coffee; symptoms improve with warmth.

Uses: bereavement and separation, emotional upset, depression, anxiety, irritating cough, sleeplessness due to shock, violent headaches or indigestion due to emotional upset, piles, hiccups, sore throat that's worse when not swallowing.

Ipecac

Symptoms: violent, persistent nausea, dislike of smell and taste of food, bluish or reddened face, sweat; symptoms occurring at regular intervals.

Uses: vomiting and nausea, dry cough, flu with chills, joint pain and nausea, gastric flu, colic, bleeding, diarrhoea, labour pains with nausea, morning sickness.

Kali bich

Symptoms: chilly, symptoms get worse in the cold, wandering pin-pointed pain.

Uses: colds and sinusitis, catarrh that's thick and stringy, headache with intermittent pain.

Lycopodium

Symptoms: poor digestion, bloating, sweet cravings, swelling, anxiety, lack of self-confidence; symptoms worst in afternoon and evening.

Uses: indigestion, nausea, constipation, flatulence, bleeding piles, cramp, throbbing headaches, chronic catarrh, dry and tickly cough, right-sided sore throat, earache, scanty urine and cystitis, night restlessness, anxiety and mood swings.

Mercurous Chloride

Symptoms: violent pain, burning, thirst, nervous exhaustion, irritability, depression.

Uses: severe cystitis, severe diarrhoea, bleeding gums, sore throat.

Nat Mur

Symptoms: dryness, extreme thirst, fever, chilliness, bitter taste in mouth, desire for salty foods, feelings of introversion and oversensitivity; symptoms are worst in the morning, in heat and after exertion but eased with rest.

Uses: migraine headaches, sensitive scalp, sweaty hands, colds with catarrh and sneezing, cold sores on lips often linked to suppressed emotions, constipation, diarrhoea, heartburn, indigestion, nausea, cracked lips and skin, swollen hands and feet from air travel, mouth ulcers, sunstroke, dizziness, water retention, suppressed emotions.

Nux vomica

Symptoms: sensitivity to cold and draughts, right-sided symptoms, workaholic, demanding and irritable; symptoms get worse after overeating or drinking, in morning and in winter but get better with heat and rest.

Uses: nausea and vomiting, morning sickness, colic, abdominal pain, indigestion, constipation, diarrhoea, piles, colds, coughs and flu, stiff, aching muscles, joint pains, cramp, fainting, hangovers, headaches, labour pains, painful menses, cystitis, nosebleeds, palpitations, insomnia, dizziness.

Phosphoric acid

Symptoms: weakness and exhaustion due to overwork or physical strain from severe diarrhoea, vomiting, bleeding or illness; symptoms get worse with cold, better with rest.

Uses: anaemia, bleeding gums, convalescence, fatigue.

Phosphorus

Symptoms: bleeding, sensitivity to cold, burning pain; symptoms get worse between dusk and midnight; affected person is often tall, slim and highly strung.

Uses: diarrhoea, fever with thirst or hunger, colds and coughs with chronic catarrh, dry skin, poor circulation in fingers, extreme perspiration under stress, fainting, sore throat and hoarseness, nausea and vomiting, profuse bleeding, nosebleeds, anaemia.

Caution: don't use if there is a history of tuberculosis.

Pulsatilla

Symptoms: dry mouth and lips, bad taste in mouth, right-sided symptoms, symptoms worst after exposure to cold, wet, wind or sun or consumption of rich, fatty food.

Uses: diarrhoea or indigestion after eating fatty, rich food, breastfeeding problems, bedwetting or stress incontinence, rattling cough, cold with yellow, smelly catarrh, chilblains, conjunctivitis, earache with discharge, sore throat, flu, one-sided fever with chills, headaches, labour pains and tearfulness, nausea and morning sickness, chickenpox, mumps, measles, feeling faint from heat, nosebleeds, teething, varicose veins especially during pregnancy, dizziness, one-sided headache.

Rhus Tox

Symptoms: aching pain, soreness, bruising, stiffness, red-tipped tongue, feelings of restlessness, irritability and fear; symptoms get worse with weather changes and better after sweating.

Uses: injuries to joints, ligaments or tissues, joint stiffness and pain, sprains and strains, swellings, headache brought on by weather change, sore throat, insomnia, skin rash, fever, exhaustion, restlessness, chickenpox, and mumps.

Ruta grav

Symptoms: soreness, bruising; symptoms worst when moving.

Uses: sprains, injuries to tendons and cartilage, wrist pain from computer use, bruised shins, pain in hands and feet, tennis elbow, headaches, eyestrain.

Sepia

Symptoms: extreme sensitivity to cold, profuse sweating, exhaustion, heaviness, yellow complexion; symptoms get worse during periods and after exertion, better after exercise or eating.

Uses: exhaustion, faintness, cramp in calf muscles, backache, constipation, cystitis, nausea from eating rich food or from the smell of certain food, travel sickness, morning sickness, abdominal tenderness, bloating and flatulence, menopausal hot flushes, sweaty feet, PMS, painful periods, thrush, toothache, insomnia with early morning waking.

Silica

Symptoms: sensitivity to cold and draughts, tiredness, night sweating, cold and smelly feet; symptoms worse in wet and damp conditions; feelings of shyness and stubbornness.

Uses: wounds slow to heal, bones slow to mend, painful inflammation, headache with forehead pain and catarrh, boils, abscesses and sties, coughs and colds, earache, tinnitus, constipation or diarrhoea, eye inflammation, sore throat, swollen glands, weak nails and hair, painful breastfeeding.

Caution: don't take if you have history of tuberculosis or surgical implants, such as breast implants, since silicea helps to expel 'foreign bodies'. If you have any sort of implant, consult a qualified practitioner for advice.

Staphisagria

Symptoms: emotional and physical sensitivity; symptoms worse after exertion and hunger; pain, aversion to tobacco smoke, feelings of humiliation, indignation and resentment.

Uses: for injuries, cuts or wounds after surgery, medical examinations, accidents, childbirth or circumcision; cystitis, bites and stings, colic, morning or travel sickness, shingles, recurring sties, shock, anger.

Sulphur

Symptoms: smelly discharges, bad breath, hot feet, extreme thirst, untidy, averse to washing, disorganised, impatient and critical; symptoms get better with fresh air and worse after baths and changes of weather.

Uses: eczema and skin rashes (not if the condition is severe), scaly skin and scalp, coughs and colds with dry nose and smelly catarrh, sore throat, earache, eye inflammation, fever, headaches, joint pain, restlessness and insomnia, burning or itching piles, diarrhoea in early morning, indigestion, measles. Do not use if there is a history of tuberculosis.

Thuja

Symptoms: bleeding, stinging, birthmarks, deep-seated conditions.

Uses: restless sleep, headaches from stress or tiredness, chronic catarrh, tooth decay, warts, scanty periods, indigestion, urinary or gynaecological infections, inflamed gums. Not to be taken during pregnancy.

Urtica Urens

Symptoms: burning, stinging, biting pain, skin irritation.

Uses: minor scalds and burns, breastfeeding problems with overabundant or insufficient flow of milk, skin rashes.

Many thanks to www.homeopathic.org and www.abchomeopathy.com for providing information for this chapter.

8
HERBAL MEDICINE

Herbal medicine must be one of the oldest branches of complementary medicine. Tribes and peoples that today live in the forests and jungles of Asia, Africa and South America have an intimate relationship with their natural surroundings and a detailed knowledge of which plants heal and even which can be used as poisons for arrow heads. So we can be sure that the first humans must have been very similar. Since the 1960s there has been a growing interest in herbal medicine and nowadays you can train to be a qualified herbalist almost anywhere in the world and probably most towns have a supplier of herbal medicine or a fully qualified herbalist.

The great thing about herbal medicine is that with a little knowledge and guidance we can make our own remedies, there is great healing power in a freshly made herbal remedy. There are almost always no side effects and unlike some traditional medicines they do not suppress symptoms but work to directly remove them or treat the root cause of the illness in a holistic way. Often a cure for a particular illness that can not be found in conventional medicine can be found in the natural world. It is also a more gentle form of healing, a cure or reduction of symptoms may take longer, perhaps even a few months, but this is because the body is being encouraged to heal in a natural way rather than a quick solution being forced upon an often already tired and troubled body or mind.

The plants that are commonly used in herbal medicine have special healing qualities that set them apart from the rest of the plant world. Of course all plants have their special place in the great scheme of nature but there seem to be a section of plants and trees that have a 'higher purpose'. We could even say they have a special energy or essence which sets them apart. If you ever have the opportunity to visit a nursery or farm that specialises in producing herbal remedies you will immediately feel that such a place has a special energy; the collection of so many healing plants in one place creates a special atmosphere, on a good day the energy is so pure that it almost feels like you are in another world. A good herbal remedy, created with a loving mind, should capture this healing energy and as well as simply acting on a physical level, they can also work on a mental and emotional level.

In this chapter you can learn how to create your own remedies and learn which remedies are suitable for different conditions, however never try to replace a conventional medicine or treat a serious condition without seeing your doctor. Combined with the other therapies in this book these remedies can have a very powerful and positive impact on your health and those you are trying to help.

MAKING YOUR OWN REMEDIES

Making your own herbal remedy is an art that can be easily learned at home with some basic knowledge and practice. When buying herbs for making your remedies it is vital that you purchase them from reputable sources. Whenever possible, grow your own herbs or buy from local growers who can provide you with information about their growing practices. Certain herbs such as nettle, dandelion and chickweed to name a few, grow abundantly in most areas and can be easily harvested. Generally using fresh herbs is most desirable, however this is not always possible and there are some herbs that are best used dried or in specific preparations. Many local health food stores and co-ops carry bulk herbs and often offer a small discount for buying in quantities of 1 pound or more.

Most dried herbs achieve the highest potency in a water base, like an infusion or tea. When making tinctures in glycerine or alcohol bases it is generally best to use fresh plant matter. However, dried roots and barks can also be used to make tinctures. When picking fresh herbs, try to pick them at their peak and after the morning dew has dried.

Herbal infusions are potent water-based preparations. They are superb for extracting the medicinal properties of dried herbs. You can drink them or use them externally as skin washes, compresses, douches, in baths, or as poultices. They are made using larger amounts of herbs and are steeped in an air-tight container for at least several hours. You can drink them at room temperature, reheated, or over ice.

Quart size canning jars are ideal to use because they rarely break when you pour boiling water into them as long as they are at room temperature when water is added. They also allow for a tight seal.

USING DRIED LEAVES

Put 1 ounce (a large handful) of dried leaves into a quart jar and fill the jar with boiling water.

Screw the lid on tight and let steep until completely cool.

Strain out plant material.

USING DRIED ROOTS OR BARKS

Put 1 ounce (a large handful) of dried roots or bark into a pint jar and fill the jar with boiling water.

Screw the lid on tight and let steep until completely cool.

Strain out plant material.

USING DRIED FLOWERS

Put 1 ounce (a large handful) of dried flowers into a quart jar and fill the jar with boiling water.

Screw the lid on tight and let steep for 2 or 3 hours.

Strain out plant material.

USING DRIED SEEDS

Put 1 ounce (a large handful) of dried seeds into a pint jar and fill the jar with boiling water.

Screw the lid on tight and let steep for half an hour - no more or the taste will be bitter. Strain out seeds.

HERBAL BATHS

When used in the bath, the medicinal properties of an herbal infusion will be absorbed through the skin. Add 2 quarts of a strained infusion to your bath water.

HERBAL POULTICES

For an herbal poultice you will retain the plant material from your infusion and apply it directly to the desired area. The liquid can be used to wash the area first if desired. This is an effective way to treat infections or wounds.

HERBAL COMPRESS

For a herbal compress you retain the plant material from an infusion and wrap it in a clean cloth or piece of gauze. Place it on desired area. You can dip it in the liquid from your infusion if desired. Compresses are useful for treating eye sties or when you don't want plant material to enter open wounds.

HERBAL TINCTURES

Herbal tinctures are potent spirit based liquid extracts. They are made using fresh plant material and liquid base such as vodka, brandy, vegetable glycerine, or even apple cider vinegar. The advantages of tinctures:

They remain potent for many years

Many doses are obtained from a small amount of plant material

They are effective in smaller doses

Some herbal compounds can only be extracted by alcohol

They are generally fast acting

Most commercial preparations are made with high proof grain alcohol. A simple and very effective choice for home use is 100 proof vodka, it's clear, affordable and easy to obtain. 100 proof means it is exactly half water and half alcohol, this makes figuring dosages easy as most dosages recommended by herbalists are based on the assumption that a tincture was made half water and half alcohol. If you are concerned about ingesting the alcohol you can place the bottle of tincture in boiling water for 1-2 minutes which will remove about half the alcohol.

HOW TO MAKE HERBAL TINCTURES

After picking your fresh herbs remove any dirty or damaged parts but don't wash them. Coarsely chop the stems, leaves and roots, flowers can be left whole. Put your herbs in a clean and dry glass jar and fill with the liquid of your choice, the herbs need to be completely immersed in the liquid. Seal the jar tightly with an airtight lid. Label your remedy with the ingredients and date and store in a dark place for 6-8 weeks, shaking occasionally. After this time strain out the herbs and pour tincture into clean, dry bottles, label with the date and ingredients used. A typical daily dose would be 15-20 drops up to a maximum of three times per day during the period of treatment. This can be varied according to the potency of the remedy and the patient's reaction, if you are unsure always start with a low dose and gradually increase it.

HERBAL OILS

Olive, coconut or almond oil are all good choices and it is best to use fresh plant material though some dried roots are appropriate provided they have been thoroughly dried. (Roots can be baked at a very low temperature for 1 hour before using.) Select fresh, dry plants, wipe off any dirt and discard damaged parts. Select enough plant material to completely fill the jar you are going to be using. Then coarsely chop the herbs and pack them into a clean and very dry jar. Use a jar with a very tight fitting lid as some herbs will produce gas. Pour your oil slowly over the herbs all the way to the very top of the jar. Poke the herbs with a long, thin object to eliminate as many air pockets as possible; this will reduce the opportunity for mould to grow. Fill with oil to the top and screw the lid on very tight. Label your jar with the date and type of herbs and oil used. Keep the jar on a flat surface at normal room temperature for 6-8 weeks, leaving the herbs in longer could result in mould. After this time pour the mixture into a clean, very dry jar and strain the herbs through a clean piece of cloth. Let the remedy sit for several days after you decant it to let any water that seeped from the herbs settle to the bottom of your jar. Pour off into a new clean, very dry jar, label your remedy and store in a cool dark place.

HERBAL SALVES

A herbal salve is easy to make at home using infused oils and beeswax. The type of salve you are making will depend on the type of infused oil you are using. Comfrey and calendula make a nice healing salve. Save small glass condiment jars and lids for storing your creations. You will need a small enamel pan, a grater, and a wooden spoon.

Heat 2 ounces of infused oil on very low heat, just until warm, add 2 tablespoons of grated beeswax and stir until completely melted and incorporated with the oil. You can also add a drop or two of essential oil at this point for fragrance. Pour the mixture into a small, shallow, glass jar and let it cool until solid. If it is too soft reheat it and add a bit more beeswax, if it is too hard reheat it and add a touch more oil. Once it is completely cool screw the lid on tight and label your remedy.

HERBAL TEAS

Herbal teabags are quite convenient to use, however the herbs must be cut quite small which compromises the quality and potency of the tea. The larger the pieces of herb the less chance there is for oxidization to occur, which reduces the healing power of the herb. You could use a tea press or brew it in a quart jar which you can strain before drinking, or use a stainless steel tea ball. If you want to treat a particular condition a maximum of three or four cups per day is advisable depending on the patient's reaction, again start with a low dose and work up.

When buying in large quantities try to check for:

COLOUR: Dried green leaves should look very close to their fresh state. Blossoms should have deep strong colour.

SMELL: The smell of dried herbs is a good indication of freshness. Look for strong, fresh aromas, you should be able to recognize the herb by smell with your eyes closed.

STORING HERBS

Store your herbs in a dark cool place in air-tight glass jars with tight fitting lids. Quart canning jars or recycled condiment jars are great for smaller quantities. A dark pantry shelf or large kitchen cupboard are ideal spots to store your herbs. Always label your jars so you don't forget what they contain. Some dried herbs can be hard to identify by sight and smell alone, though eventually you will be able to recognize the subtle distinguishing qualities of your favourites.

COMMONLY USED HERBAL REMEDIES

Here is a list of the most commonly used herbs which you can easily obtain from health shops, on the internet, or you will be able to grow/harvest some yourself:

Agnus Castus

The medicine is made from fresh or dried berries and taken as tablets or a liquid tincture.

Uses: Menstrual irregularity, PMS, menopause, promotes breast milk in nursing mothers, boosts fertility.

Note: Not recommended during pregnancy. Avoid if taking progesterone drugs.

Aloe Vera

The medicine is made from gel inside the leaves and taken as a gel applied directly or drunk as juice.

Uses: Gel can be applied topically to ease minor burns, scalds, cuts and sunburn. Liquid form can be drunk to soothe the digestive system and protect against ulcers. Bitter aloes, the bitter liquid exuded from the leaf, can be used to treat constipation.

Note: Not recommended during pregnancy. Bitter aloes shouldn't be applied to the skin or taken if suffering from kidney disease or haemorrhoids.

Black Cohosh

The medicine is made from fresh or dried roots and taken as tablets or liquid tincture.

Uses: Traditional Native American remedy for menstrual pain and menopausal hot flushes. Also used to ease arthritic and rheumatic pain due to inflammation and to treat high blood pressure, tinnitus, asthma and whooping cough.

Note: Not recommended during pregnancy or while breastfeeding.

Buchu

The medicine is made from the leaves and taken as an infusion or liquid tincture.

Uses: Traditional remedy of the Khoikhoin people of South Africa for treating urinary infections such as cystitis and urethritis. Also used for prostate inflammation, fluid retention and vaginal thrush.

Note: Not recommended during pregnancy or while breastfeeding.

Cat's Claw

The medicine is made from the inner bark and roots and taken as tablets, tincture, herbal tea or cream.

Uses: Traditional Peruvian remedy for boosting the immune system to treat and prevent infection. Also used for gastrointestinal disorders such as ulcers, diverticulitis or gastritis, viral and bacterial infections, skin allergies and rheumatoid arthritis.

Note: Although no serious adverse reactions have been reported, it's best avoided by pregnant and breastfeeding women.

Calendula

The medicine is made from the leaves and flowers and taken as a tincture, infusion, or cream.

Uses: Period pains, digestive irritation, colds, coughs and viruses. Applied externally for skin problems including nappy rash, varicose veins, cuts and grazes, chilblains, fungal infections and insect stings; also used for mouth ulcers.

Note: Not recommended during pregnancy.

Chamomile

The medicine is made from the fresh or dried flower heads and taken as an infusion, taken as a tea or as a cream.

Uses: Indigestion and irritable bowel syndrome, nervous tension, insomnia, PMS, skin conditions such as eczema, colic and teething problems in babies and young children, hay fever, bronchitis, catarrh, asthma.

Note: The fresh plant can cause skin rash or irritation. The essential oil isn't recommended during pregnancy.

Comfrey

The medicine is made from the roots and leaves and taken as a cream/ointment, compress, liquid tincture or as a tea.

Uses: Used externally for thousands of years to heal bruises, sprains, fractures, broken bones and skin problems such as acne, boils, scars and rashes. Taken internally for stomach ulcers and respiratory problems.

Note: Use is restricted in some countries. Root shouldn't be taken internally. Oil from the leaves shouldn't be applied to open wounds.

Cranberry

The medicine is made from the berries and taken as powder, tablet or juice.

Uses: Urinary infections, such as cystitis (prevents harmful bacteria adhering to the walls of the bladder or urinary tract).

Note: Not recommended for those suffering from kidney disease without professional advice.

Devil's claw

The medicine is made from the dried tubers and taken as tablets or liquid tincture.

Uses: Arthritis, gout, stiff joints, back pain, skin inflammation, sores and boils. Traditional South African remedy for digestive problems, especially gall bladder or stomach.

Note: Not to be taken during pregnancy or by people with a stomach or duodenal ulcer.

Dong quai

The medicine is made from the roots and taken as tablets or liquid tincture.

Uses: Irregular menstruation, PMS, menopausal symptoms, cramps, restores health after childbirth, blood tonic.

Note: Not recommended during pregnancy or for those with diabetes. High doses may cause abdominal bloating and changes in menstrual timing or flow.

Echinacea

The medicine is made from the roots, flowers and seeds and taken as tablet/capsule, liquid tincture, or cream.

Uses: To prevent and fight infections, especially colds, flu, coughs and sore throats. Can be helpful for chronic fatigue syndrome, allergic conditions such as asthma and hay fever, shingles, herpes and mouth ulcers, or applied topically for eczema, boils or acne.

Note: Rare, but high doses (over 1,000mg) can sometimes cause dizziness or nausea. For the best effect, it shouldn't be taken for more than one to two weeks at a time.

Eyebright

The medicine is made from the aerial parts and taken as tablets or liquid tincture.

Uses: Eye tonic for eye irritation or infections such as conjunctivitis, sties and eyestrain. Also used internally for sinusitis, catarrh, sore throats and hay fever.

Note: None known, although its safety during pregnancy hasn't been proven.

Feverfew

The medicine is made from the leaves and aerial parts and taken as fresh leaves, tablets/capsules or liquid tincture.

Uses: Migraine, irregular or painful periods, joint inflammation and pain, fevers, childbirth.

Note: Not to be taken during pregnancy or if taking warfarin or any other blood-thinning medication. Eating the fresh leaves can trigger mouth ulcers in some people.

Garlic

The medicine is made from the bulbs and taken as food, rubbed on skin, tablets or capsules.

Uses: Colds, flu, coughs, sinusitis and chest infections, candida albicans, high blood pressure and heart disease, circulatory problems, skin problems including acne and impetigo, blood sugar regulation, digestive infections.

Note: Not to be taken with anti-clotting medication. If you're breastfeeding, you may find that garlic makes your baby's colic worse.

Ginger

The medicine is made from the oil of the root and taken as raw food or cooked, or as an infusion, capsules or liquid tincture.

Uses: Travel sickness, morning sickness or nausea, indigestion, colds and flu, chilblains and arthritis. Also helps to lower blood pressure.

Note: Not to be taken by those suffering from peptic ulcers. The essential oil shouldn't be taken internally without professional supervision. Long-term use in pregnancy isn't recommended.

Ginkgo Biloba

The medicine is made from the leaves and nuts and taken as tablet/capsule, liquid tincture, or infusion.

Uses: Poor memory and concentration and impaired mental function, high blood pressure, stroke, varicose veins, piles, asthma, wheezing.

Note: High doses (over 120mg a day) can cause headaches. Not usually recommended for children and not to be taken by those on blood-thinning medication.

Ginseng

The medicine is made from the roots and taken as tablets/capsules or liquid tincture.

Uses: Stress, nervous exhaustion, insomnia, depression, poor memory and concentration, chronic fatigue syndrome, jet lag.

Note: Not to be taken with coffee or for more than six weeks at a time. Avoid if pregnant or have high blood pressure. Unsuitable for children.

Golden seal

The medicine is made from the fresh or dried rhizome and taken as capsules or liquid tincture.

Uses: Traditional Cherokee remedy for wounds and ulcers. Used for digestive disorders such as heartburn, dyspepsia and indigestion, catarrh, ear, mouth, sinus and throat infections, PMS and menstrual discomfort, urinary infections and candida.

Note: Not to be taken if pregnant, breastfeeding or suffering from high blood pressure.

Hawthorn

The medicine is made from the flowers and berries and taken as tablets, decoction or liquid tincture.

Uses: Heart disease (including angina and coronary artery disease), high blood pressure, poor memory, nervous tension, insomnia.

Note: Those with heart disease and pregnant or breastfeeding women should seek professional advice before taking hawthorn.

Juniper

The medicine is made from the berries and twigs and taken as tablets or infusions.

Uses: Urinary infections such as cystitis, water retention, rheumatism, chest problems.

Note: Avoid if pregnant. Don't use internally for more than six weeks.

Milk thistle

The medicine is made from the seeds and flower heads and taken as capsules, decoction or liquid tincture.

Uses: Liver disorders including hepatitis, cirrhosis and jaundice, PMS, candidiasis, psoriasis.

Nettle

The medicine is made from the aerial parts and roots and taken as infusion, decoction, tincture or ointment.

Uses: Elimination of waste products, arthritis, gout, urinary problems, hay fever, allergies, eczema, bleeding, ear, nose and throat problems.

Note: Occasional allergic reactions.

Passion flower

The medicine is made from the aerial parts and flowers and taken as infusion, tincture, or tablets.

Uses: Anxiety, stress, insomnia, cramps, toothache, menstrual pain, headache.

Note: Can cause drowsiness, so caution is needed when driving or handling machinery. Avoid high doses when pregnant.

Peppermint

The medicine is made from the leaves and taken as an infusion or capsules.

Uses: Digestive problems, especially indigestion, heartburn, colic and flatulence. Also helps nausea, tension headaches and migraine, respiratory infections, fevers and travel sickness.

Note: Not suitable for pregnant or nursing women, or children under 12. The essential oil shouldn't be taken internally without professional supervision.

Red clover

The medicine is made from the flowers and taken as tablets, liquid tincture or infusion.

Uses: Coughs, bronchitis, eczema, sores, scrofula (TB of the neck) and as a gargle for mouth ulcers and sore throats. Also relieves menopausal symptoms.

Note: Should be avoided by pregnant and breastfeeding women.

St John's Wort

The medicine is made from the flowers and aerial parts and taken as capsule, infusion, liquid tincture or cream.

Uses: Depression, anxiety, insomnia, viral infections, menstrual cramps, menopausal stress, insect bites, burns, neuralgia, cramp.

Note: Exposure to sun should be avoided. Not to be taken with the contraceptive pill, anti-epilepsy treatments and a number of other medications including antidepressants.

Sarsaparilla

The medicine is made from the roots and rhizome and taken as tablets, infusion or tincture.

Uses: Skin problems, especially irritated skin, psoriasis and eczema, rheumatism.

Saw palmetto

The medicine is made from the berries and taken as tablets or infusion.

Uses: Urinary problems, prostate problems, impotence and low libido, building up the body.

Schizandra

The medicine is made from the fruit and taken an infusion, tincture, decoction or capsules.

Uses: Liver problems such as hepatitis, stress, anxiety, insomnia, allergic skin conditions such as hives, recovery after surgery, aids athletic endurance, improves sexual function.

Note: Occasionally causes heartburn. Some studies suggest that epileptics and those with hypertension should avoid it or use it with great caution.

Slippery elm

The medicine is made from the bark and taken as infusion, capsules or poultice.

Uses: Digestive problems such as indigestion, gastritis, ulcers, dyspepsia, colitis, constipation and irritable bowel syndrome. Also used for sore throats, bronchitis, coughs, urinary problems and skin conditions such as boils.

Uva Ursi (Bearberry)

The medicine is made from the leaves and taken as tablet, infusion or decoction.

Uses: Urinary tract disorders such as cystitis, urethritis, fluid retention and bedwetting. Also profuse bleeding during menstruation, diarrhoea and toothache.

Note: not to be used during pregnancy or while breastfeeding. Shouldn't be used for more than two weeks at a time without professional supervision. Higher doses occasionally lead to nausea.

Valerian

The medicine is made from the roots and rhizome and taken as tablets, decoction or tincture.

Uses: Insomnia, nervous tension, stress, neuralgia, PMS, menstrual cramps and high blood pressure.

Note: Can cause drowsiness. Shouldn't be taken with sleep medication.

Wild Yam

The medicine is made from the roots and tubers and taken as tincture, cream or decoction.

Uses: Traditional North and Central American native remedy for painful periods, cramps and labour. Also used for menopausal symptoms, arthritis and rheumatism, joint inflammation, colic, irritable bowel syndrome and muscle spasms.

Note: Not to be taken during pregnancy.

COMMON AILMENTS THAT CAN BE TREATED WITH HERBAL REMEDIES.

It is important to consult your doctor or a qualified herbalist before treating a serious condition. Most of the following herbs can be bought from a health store, it is important to follow the instructions carefully and do not try to replace a conventional medicine without consulting your doctor.

Abscess
Echinacea, Garlic, Marshmallow.

ACNE
Blue Flag, Cleavers, Echinacea, Garlic, Poke Root.

ADENOIDS
Cleavers, Echinacea, Garlic, Golden Seal, Marigold, Poke Root, Wild Indigo.

ANGINA
Hawthorn.

ANXIETY
Californian Poppy, Chamomile,
Mother Wort, Skullcap, Valerian, Wild Lettuce.

APPENDICITIS
Agrimony, American Cranesbill, Golden Seal, Wild Yam.

APPETITE LOSS

Calamus, Centaury, Condurango, Gentian, Mugwort, Wormwood.

ARTERIOSCLEROSIS

Lime, Hawthorn, Mistletoe.

ARTHRITIS

Black Cohosh, Bogbean, Celery Seed, Guaiacum, Prickly Ash, Wild Yam.

ASTHMA

Elecampane, Ephedra, Grindelia, Lobelia, Pill-bearing Spurge, Sundew, Wild Cherry.

BLOOD PRESSURE (HIGH)

Hawthorn, Lime Blossom, Mistletoe, Yarrow, Balm, Black Haw, Cramp Bark, Garlic.

BOILS

Blue Flag, Echinacea, Garlic, Myrrh, Pasque Flower, Poke Root, Wild Indigo.

BRONCHITIS

Blood Root, Coltsfoot, Echinacea, Elecampane, Garlic, Grindelia, Lobelia, Mouse Ear, Mullein, Pill-bearing Spurge, Pleurisy Root, Senega, Sundew, White Horehound.

BRUISES

Arnica, Elder, Chickweed, Cucumber, Lady's Mantle, Marigold,

St John's Wort.

BURNS

Aloe, Elder, Marigold, Greater Plantain, St John's Wort, Chamomile, Duckweed, Comfrey, Cucumber, Quince Seed.

CATARRH

Echinacea, Elder, Eyebright, Garlic, Golden Rod, Golden Seal, Mouse Ear, Mullein, Peppermint, Pine, Poke Root.

CIRCULATION

Cayenne, Ginger, Prickly Ash, Black Mustard, Horseradish, Rosemary.

COLDS

Angelica, Cayenne, Elder, Garlic, Ginger, Golden Rod, Golden Seal, Hyssop, Peppermint, Yarrow.

COLIC

Angelica, Boldo, Calamus, Condurango, Cramp Bark, Gentian, Ginger, Peppermint, Valerian.

COLITIS

Agrimony, American Cranesbill.

CONJUNCTIVITIS

Chamomile, Eyebright, Golden Seal.

CONSTIPATION

Balmony, Barberry, Buckthorn, Cascara Sagrada, Rhubarb Root, Senna, Yellow Dock.

COUGH

Angelica, Aniseed, Balm of Gilead, Coltsfoot, Comfrey, Cowslip, Elecampane, Garlic, Golden Seal, Grindelia, Hyssop, Mouse Ear, Pine, Greater Plantain.

CRAMP

Black Cohosh, Cramp Bark, Pasque, Flower, Skullcap, Valerian, Wild Lettuce, Wild Yam.

CYSTITIS

Bearberry, Buchu, Couchgrass, Echinacea, Juniper, Yarrow.

DEPRESSION

Damiana, Kola, Oats, Skullcap, Wormwood, Balm, Celery, Chamomile, Mistletoe, Mugwort, Rosemary, Southernwood, Valerian, St John's Wort.

DIARRHEA

For Adults - Agrimony, American Cranesbill, Barberry, Black Catechu, Comfrey, Lady's Mantle, Meadowsweet, Greater Plantain. For Children - Meadowsweet.

DIVERTICULITIS

Wild yam, Comfrey, Chamomile, Marshmallow.

ECZEMA

Blue Flag, Burdock, Duckweed, Cleavers, Figwort, Golden Seal, Nettles, Yellow Dock.

FEVER

Boneset, Catnip, Cayenne, Ginger, Peruvian Bark, Pleurisy Root.

FIBROSITIS

Cayenne, Ginger, Ragwort, Wintergreen, Horseradish, Rosemary, St John's Wort.

FLATULENCE

Angelica, Calamus, Caraway, Cardamon, Cayenne, Cinnamon, Condurango, Coriander, Fennel, Gentian.

FUNGUS INFECTION

Marigold, Golden Seal, Greater Celandine, Myrrh.

GALL-BLADDER PROBLEMS

Balmony, Black Root, Dandelion, Fringetree Bark, Milk Thistle.

GASTRITIS

American Cranesbill, Calamus, Comfrey, Golden Seal, Marshmallow, Meadowsweet.

GINGIVITIS

Bistort, Echinacea, Golden Seal, Myrrh, Oak Bark, Poke Root, Rhatany.

GLANDS (SWOLLEN)

Cleavers, Echinacea, Poke Root.

GLANDULAR FEVER

Echinacea, Myrrh, Poke Root, Wormwood, Garlic.

HALITOSIS

Dill, Fennel.

HAYFEVER

Ephedra, Golden Seal, Elder, Eyebright, Garlic, Peppermint.

HEADACHE

Betony, Feverfew, Marjoram.

HEARTBURN

Iceland Moss, Irish Moss, Mallow, Slippery Elm.

HYPERSENSITIVITY

Ephedra.

INCONTINENCE (URINARY)

Ephedra, Horsetail, Agrimony.

INDIGESTION

Balm, Calamus, Cayenne, Centaury, Chamomile, Condurango, Fennel, Ginger, Peppermint, Pierian, Wild Yam, Wormwood.

INFECTION
Cleavers, Echinacea, Garlic, Golden Seal.

INFLUENZA
Boneset, Cayenne, Echinacea, Garlic, Golden Seal, Pleurisy Root.

INSOMNIA
Californian Poppy, Hops, Jamaican Flower, Valerian, Wild Lettuce.

ITCHING
Chickweed, Golden Seal.

JAUNDICE
Balmony, Barberry, Black Root, Dandelion, Vervain, Yellow Dock.

KIDNEY STONES
Bearberry, Corn Silk, Couchgrass, Gravel Root, Hydrangea, Stone Roof.

LABOUR PAINS - FALSE
Black Cohosh, Cramp Bark, Motherwort, Wild Yam.

LARYNGITIS
Balm of Gilead, Blood Root, Echinacea, Golden Seal.

LIVER PROBLEMS
Bahnony, Black Root, Blue Flag, Centaury, Dandelion, Yellow Dock.

LUMBAGO
Black Mustard, Cayenne, Ragwort, Wintergreen.

MENOPAUSE
Black Cohosh, Chaste Tree, False Unicorn Root, Golden Seal, St John's Wort.

MENSTRUATION - DELAYED
Blue Cohosh, Chaste Tree, False Unicorn Root, Life Root, Parsley, Marigold, Motherwort, Mugwort, Thuja, Yarrow.

MENSTRUATION (EXCESSIVE)
American Cranesbill, Beth, Root, Periwinkle, Golden Seal, Lady's Mantle.

MENSTRUATION - PAINFUL
Black Cohosh. Black Haw, Jamaican Dogwood, Pasque Flower, St John's Wort, Skullcap, Valerian, Wild Lettuce, Blue Cohosh, Butterbur, Caraway, Chaste Tree, False Unicorn Root, Marigold, Squaw Vine, Wild Yam.

MIGRAINE
Feverfew, Jamaican Dogwood, Kola, Mistletoe, Peppermint, Skullcap, Wormwood.

MILK STIMULATION - BREAST
Coat's Rue, Milk Thistle, Borage, Caraway, Dill, Fennel, Fenugreek.

MISCARRIAGE - THREATENED

Blue Cohosh, False Unicorn Root, Black Haw, Cramp Bark.

MOUTH ULCERS

Myrrh, Red Sage, Bistort, Chamomile, Lady's Mantle.

NAUSEA

Black Horehound, Chamomile, Meadowsweet, Peppermint, Avens, Cayenne, Cinnamon, Cloves, Fennel, Galangal, Marshmallow.

NEURALGIA

Betony, Black Cohosh, Jamaican Dogwood, Mistletoe, Passion Flower, St John's Wort, Skullcap, Valerian, Hops, Pasque Flower, Rosemary.

NOSEBLEED

Lady's Mantle, Witch Hazel, Marigold, Tormentil.

OVARIAN PAIN

Jamaican Dogwood, Pasque Flower, Valerian, Passion Flower, St John's Wort, Skullcap, Wild Yam.

PAIN

Black Cohosh, Black Willow, Jamaican Dogwood, Valerian, Wild Lettuce, Cramp Bark, Hops, Rosemary, Skullcap.

PALPITATIONS

Motherwort, Skullcap, Valerian.

PHLEBITIS

Hawthorn, Horsechestnut, Lime Blossom, Mistletoe.

PREGNANCY TONIC

Raspberry Leaves, Squaw Vine.

PREGNANCY - VOMITING

Black Horehound, False Unicorn Root, Meadowsweet, Blue Cohosh, Peppermint.

PRE-MENSTRUAL TENSION

Chaste Tree, Skullcap, Valerian, Lime Blossom, Pasque Flower.

PROSTATE

Damiana, Horsetail, Hydrangea, Saw Palmetto, Corn Silk, Couchgrass, Sea Holly.

PSORIASIS

Blue Flag, Burdock, Cleavers, Mountain Grape, Red Clover, Sarsaparilla, Yellow Dock, Balm of Gilead, Chickweed, Flax Seed, Sassafras, Thuja.

RHEUMATISM

Angelica, Black Cohosh, Bogbean, Celery Seed, Guaiacum, Meadowsweet, Prickly Ash, White Poplar, Wild Lettuce, Wild Yam, Yarrow, Arnica, Bittersweet, Black Mustard, Blue Cohosh, Burdock, Cayenne, Couchgrass.

SCIATICA

Black Cohosh, Jamaican Dogwood, St John's Wort, Yarrow.

SHINGLES

Jamaican Dogwood, Mistletoe, Passion Flower, St John's Wort, Flax Seed, Hops, Skullcap, Valerian, Wild Lettuce, Wild Yam.

SINUSITIS

Elder, Eyebright, Garlic, Golden Rod, Golden Seal, Poke Root, Scots Pine, Wild Indigo, Chamomile, Myrrh, Peppermint, Thyme, Yarrow.

SORETHROAT

Balm of Gilead, Echinacea, Garlic, Golden Seal, Oak, Agrimony, Bayberry, Cayenne, Chamomile, Ginger, Golden Rod, Myrrh, Poke Root, Silverweed, Thyme.

SPOTS

Blue Flag, Cleavers, Echinacea, Figwort, Garlic, Poke Root.

STRESS

Damiana, Lime Blossom, Mistletoe, St John's Wort, Skullcap, Balm, Betony, Borage, Chamomile, Cowslip, Hops, Oats. Pasque Flower, Passion Flower, Valerian, Wild Lettuce, Wormwood.

SUNBURN

Aloe, Marigold, Eyebright, St John's Wort.

TENSION

Betony, Cowslip, Jamaiccm Dogwood, Lime Blossom, Mistletoe, Motherwort, Pasque Floirer, Passion Flower, St John's Wort, Skullcap, Valerian, Vervain, Wild Lettuce, Balm, Californian Poppy, Damiana, Hops, Peppermint.

TINNITUS

Black Cohosh, Golden Seal, Golden Rod, Ground Ivy.

TONSILLITIS

Cleavers, Echinacea, Garlic, Golden Seal, Myrrh, Poke Root, Red Sage, Thyme, Wild Indigo.

TOOTHACHE

Cloves.

TRAVEL SICKNESS

Black Horehound, Galangal, Peppermint.

TUMOURS

Cleavers, Comfrey, Elder, Fenugreek, Greater Celandine, Red Clover, Sweet Violet, Thuja.

ULCERS (PEPTIC)

American Cranesbill, Comfrey, Marshmallow, Meadowsweet, Slippery Elm, Calamus, Golden Seal, Irish Moss, Liquorice, Mallow.

ULCERS (SKIN)

Chickweed, Comfrey, Golden Seal, Marigold, Echinacea, Marshmallow.

VARICOSE ULCERS

Golden Seal, Horsechestnut, Marigold, Comfrey, Marshmallow.

VARICOSE VEINS

Horsechestnut, Hawthorn, Lime Blossom, St John's Wort, Witch Hazel.

VOMITING

Black Horehound, Meadowsweet, Cinnamon, Cloves, Comfrey, False Unicorn Root, Iceland Moss, Peppermint, Rosemary.

WARTS

Greater Celandine, Thuja.

WATER RETENTION

Bearberry, Broom, Buchu, Dandelion, Gravel Root, Jumper Berries, Wild Carrot, Burr-Marigold, Celery Seed, Corn Silk, Horsetail, Parsley, Sea Holly, Silver Birch, Stone Root, Yarrow.

WHOOPING COUGH

Coltsfoot, Grindelia, Lobelia, Mouse Ear, Black Cohosh, Ephedra, Garlic, Mullein, Pansy, Red Clover, Sundew, Wild Cherry.

WORMS

Cucumber, Garlic, Kousso, Male Fern, Pomegranate, Pumpkin, Quassia, Santonica, Tansy, Wormwood.

WOUNDS

Chickweed, Comfrey, Elder, Golden Seal, Marigold, Greater Plantain, St John's Wort, Self-Heal, Woundwort, Carline Thistle, Chamomile, Fenugreek, Garlic, Horsetail, Lady's Mantle, Marshmallow, Mouse Ear, Red- Sage.

Many thanks to www.herbalremediesinfo.com for providing information for this chapter.

9
CRYSTAL THERAPY

Crystal healing has become more accepted as a mainstream healing therapy in recent years. This is mainly related to the increased availability of crystals and an increasing awareness of their healing properties. If you are in any doubt about the power of crystals all you have to do is to buy a small piece of clear quartz and carry it in your pocket for a few days, then leave it at home for a day and you will notice that life is a little tougher without it! Some people feel increased energy, clarity of mind and strengthening of purpose or confidence; try it for yourself and see what you feel. Another way to feel the special power that crystals hold is to meditate with them or just lie down somewhere quiet and comfortable, maybe outside if it is warm, and place the crystal on your body. An even simpler way to feel the energy created by crystals is to visit a crystal shop; just spend a few minutes walking round and you will feel something in the atmosphere.

The healing life force energies crystals hold can be utilised by wearing them as jewellery, keeping them loose in your pocket or having them around your home. There are also many qualified and experienced crystal healers you can visit for a treatment. They will place crystals around and on the body of a patient, and they will use specific crystals in certain areas depending on the problem being treated. The colour of the crystal also plays a big part in the healing process and may correspond to an associated chakra.

If our life force energies are out of balance we can experience different problems including ill health, lack of well-being, depression, stress, tiredness, lack of self-esteem, etc. Physical, mental and emotional discomfort is often related to blocked or low life force energy in the body. To be healthy we need a high or pure level of energy vibration in all areas of our physical and energetic body. If something enters the body which irritates the system, such as bad food entering our digestive system, or we experience a stressful situation which disturbs our mind, the result is a slowing down in the normal vibrational pattern of the energetic body which can cause illness. If our inner energies are depleted we are more susceptible to negative energies and harmful environmental influences which can cause more energy blockages and the cycle of poor health can become self-perpetuating.

As well as helping the healing process, crystals can be an extremely valuable aid in helping us cope with the rigors of daily life. Each crystal and gemstone has its own vibrational quality. The energy that they transmit can have a powerful effect on the different energy vibrations in a human being and when used correctly can balance, harmonise and attune mind, body, and spirit. Through this balancing and attuning, they give us the ability to heal ourselves firstly on an energetic level and then on a mental, emotional and physical level.

Crystals will need to be cleansed sometimes by holding them under running water or immersing them in salt water. As you do this hold the intention in your mind that all the negativity will be washed away. You can also place your crystals in sun or moonlight for a few hours. There are a few crystals that never require cleaning like citrine, kyanite and azeztulite; they are self cleaning, whilst clear quartz and carnelian can cleanse other crystals.

It is possible to programme the energy of a crystal through the power of thought and intention. Firstly hold the crystal in your hand and picture light surrounding it, then set an intention like 'this is a healing crystal that can only work for the greatest good of all' or something similar that you think is appropriate. You can be more specific and think something like 'this crystal is programmed to bring inner peace and contentment' or you can relate your intention to a particular illness like 'this crystal is programmed to relieve arthritis'. Following that place your crystal where you will see it frequently, alternatively carry it around with you. At least hold the crystal a few times during the day. You could sit down for a few minutes and imagine the healing energies of the crystal entering your body. Regular cleansing and re-programming of the crystal will make the process more powerful.

For physical, mental and emotional problems, and for your general health and well-being regularly use crystals in the following ways:

- Balance your chakras with coloured crystals
- Place crystals within your aura, in your pocket or around the room
- Wear your crystals
- Use different crystals with different healing methods, like Reiki and Reflexology, you can massage some of the reflex points with a crystal
- Use crystals to help you to be more positive
- Protect yourself from negative influences in the environment
- Clear out emotional baggage
- Meditate and use affirmations with crystals
- Crystals can keep the energy healthy in your home and workplace

There are seven main energy centres or chakras in the body, one of the main aims of crystal healing is to energise and bring them all in to balance. Each chakra has a different colour and vibrational frequency, when there is some physical, emotional or mental illness this will relate to at least one of the corresponding chakras being out of balance in some way. Crystals have a vibrational quality that can bring the chakra back in to harmony with the whole body system. The crystal placement diagram below indicates where they can be placed, but use your instincts to get the exact position for you or your patient. You can also place crystals around the body in the area of the aura and hold crystals in each hand, but it is best to start with the simple placement described below.

Lie comfortably in a warm and relaxing environment and position crystals as follows:

Base Chakra	Hematite	Base of spine
Sacral Chakra	Carnelian	Below navel
Solar Plexus Chakra	Citrine	Just below ribcage
Heart Chakra	Rose Quartz	Centre of chest
Throat Chakra	Sodalite	Top of breast bone
Brow Chakra	Amethyst	Centre of forehead
Crown Chakra	Rutilated Quartz	Top/Back of head

This diagram shows the position and colour of the charkas:

crystal placement

crown
brow
throat
heart
solar plexus
sacral
base

Hematite - Base Chakra

Grounding, helps prevent feelings of faintness and dizziness; good for self-control; aids memory; helps with concentration for detailed work or study; aids willpower; lessens the effects of jet lag; can help in alleviating stress and promoting sound sleep.

Carnelian - Base/Sacral Chakra

Aids concentration; helps assertiveness without leading to aggression; helps with determining one's feelings; can prevent feelings of fear, envy and sadness.

Citrine - Solar Plexus Chakra

Uplifting; promotes emotional and mental clarity; helps reduce anxiety, fear and depression; increases self-esteem and reduces self-destructive tendencies; good for problem solving, memory, confidence and optimism.

Rose Quartz - Heart Chakra

Balancing the emotions; uplifts the spirits; discourages negative thoughts; boosts self-esteem and confidence; helps to heal the emotions following loss or hurt; relaxing and helps alleviate stress.

Sodalite - Brow/Throat Chakra

Good for communication - ideas, writing and logic; repels effects of electro-magnetic fields; balances energy through thyroid and pituitary glands; helps with insomnia.

Amethyst - Brow Chakra

Aids creative thinking; relieves insomnia; helpful in grief; aids meditation; spiritually uplifting; helps prevent nightmares and creates inspiring dreams; calms anger and impatience; helpful in overcoming addictions.

Rutilated Quartz - Crown Chakra

Amplifies energy, both physical and mental; helps with deep thought processes such as meditation, insight and clairvoyance; boosts immune system and general physical strength.

Here is a list of widely available crystals and gems which can be used for healing and personal growth. You should be able to obtain them from a local crystal supplier or from one of the many online suppliers.

Agate

A soothing and calming crystal. Releases stress, brings relaxation and helps to stop worrying.

Green Aventurine

For calming anxiety and fears. Helps to develop decisiveness and to amplify leadership qualities.

Blue Chalcedony

Improves the memory, increases mental flexibility and enhances listening and communication skills. It can also encourage an optimistic outlook on life.

Orange Calcite

An energizing stone, it balances the emotions, reduces fear, dissolves problems and maximises potential.

Carnelian

A stone of life force and energy. It is said to increase ambition, drive and confidence and to protect the wearer against negative emotions.

Chrysocolla

A tranquil and sustaining stone. It brings acceptance and peace of mind, inspires creativity and encourages compassion and nurturing.

Chrysoprase

This stone clarifies problems, stimulates creativity and draws out inner talents. Its gentle, relaxing energy can also encourage sleep and relaxation.

Citrine

A 'feel good' gemstone. It aids emotional well-being, creativity, decisiveness and attracts abundance on all levels.

Fluorite

Brings order and helps with learning and absorbing new ideas. It attracts harmony and tranquillity and is said to provide protection against colds and flu.

Garnet

The stone of health and life force. It is linked to an enhanced love life, sex drive and good health and vitality.

Haematite

A grounding crystal. Believed to enhance reliability and willpower, remove self-limitations and to impart confidence. It can inspire you while keeping your feet firmly on the ground.

Green Jade

Promotes love, courage, justice and wisdom. It is believed to calm the nervous system and to channel passion in constructive ways.

Mookaite Jasper

An emotional protector helping you to block unwanted outside influences. It can also aid you in adapting to and accepting change and is particularly sustaining in times of stress.

Ocean Jasper

Encourages self-love and a love of others. It is a good emotional healer and can bring peace of mind and tranquillity.

Red Jasper

A gently stimulating crystal and is said to allow insight into difficult situations. It makes an excellent 'worry bead' as it calms the emotions when handled.

Labradorite

Sometimes called the 'Stone of Destiny' as it helps you to find your true path. It also promotes wisdom, understanding and patience and deflects unwanted energies.

Lapis Lazuli

Encourages self-knowledge and self-expression. A powerful thought amplifier, stimulating the higher levels of the mind, bringing clarity and objectivity.

Moldavite

A rare stone with a powerful energy. It is said to enhance psychic abilities and to help manifest positive life changes.

Moonstone

Enhances feminine qualities, gentleness, receptivity, intuition and psychic powers and it seals and protects the energy field.

Opalite

Calming and relaxing, it stabilizes mood swings and enhances psychic powers.

Peridot

For protecting and cleansing. Its clear fresh energy rejuvenates the whole body and it can alleviate jealousy and resentment while enhancing confidence and assertion.

Pink Smithsonite

For tranquillity, charm, kindness and favourable outcomes. It is a comforting and soothing crystal that can form a buffer against life's problems.

Clear Quartz

A powerful healing crystal. It can be used to amplify healing energy, bring the body into balance and to stabilize and strengthen the body's energy field. Wearing or holding clear Quartz is said to promote clarity of thought.

Rose Quartz

Encourages forgiveness and compassion and helps us let go of anger resentment and jealousy. It brings deep inner healing and self-love and is excellent for use in times of emotional stress.

Rhodonite

A crystal for emotional healing. It can clear away emotional wounds and scars from the past and allow you to achieve your highest potential.

Selenite

A calming crystal, bringing deep peace and a lightness of being.

Sodalite

Brings joy to a heavy heart. It encourages self-esteem, self-acceptance and self-trust. It can help eliminate mental confusion and encourage rational thought.

Sunstone

The stone of leadership, it encourages self-empowerment, originality, independence and vitality and is said to bring good luck and abundance.

Tiger's Eye

For grounding and uplifting. It promotes a positive attitude, laughter and humour, and it is said to attract prosperity, wealth and success.

Blue Topaz

Brings calm and serenity. It helps you tap into inner resources, discover and successfully achieve your goals. It is a useful stone to help you tackle a problem or confusing thoughts or feelings.

Green Tourmaline

A nurturing crystal, which is believed to inspire creativity, attract abundance and encourage a joy of life.

Tourmaline

A powerful mental healer. It is said to balance the right and left hemispheres of the brain and to change negative thought patterns into positive ones.

Turquoise

A protective crystal. It can help calm the nerves when speaking in public, stabilise mood swings, bring inner clam, and allow self-expression. It is said to help you find your true path in life.

Many thanks to www.mindstones.com for providing information for this chapter.

10
YOGA

Yoga is an exercise system, a way of life and a self healing therapy. Learning a healing exercise technique like yoga or tai chi is very empowering, we are really doing something good for ourselves rather than relying on a therapist. Such techniques are also excellent preventative medicine. To understand what yoga is all about, you need to experience it for yourself. At first glance it may seem to be just a series of strange physical postures which keep the body lean and flexible. But in time, anyone who continues with regular practice becomes aware of a subtle change in their approach to life. Yoga helps you discover your true nature, a state of inner peace, through the practice of toning and relaxing your body at the same time as relaxing your mind.

The beginnings of yoga were developed in Northern India over 5,000 years ago. The word yoga was first mentioned in the oldest sacred texts, the Rig Veda. The Vedas were a collection of texts containing songs and rituals used by Brahmans, the Vedic priests. Yoga was slowly refined and developed by Vedic priests who documented their practices and beliefs in the *Upanishads*, a huge work containing over 200 scriptures. The most renowned of these Yogic scriptures is the *Bhagavad-Gita*, composed around 500 BC. The *Upanishads* teach a path to inner peace through the reduction of the ego which comes with self-knowledge. The first systematic presentation of yoga was Patanjali's Yoga Sutras. Written some time in the second century, this text describes the path of Raja Yoga, often called 'classical yoga'. Patanjali organized the practice of yoga into an 'eight limbed path' containing the steps and stages towards obtaining Samadhi or enlightenment. Patanjali is often considered the father of yoga and his sutras still strongly influence all styles of modern yoga.

A few centuries after Patanjali, yoga masters created a system of practices designed to rejuvenate the body and prolong life. They also developed Tantra Yoga, with radical techniques to cleanse the body and mind in order to break the knots that bind us to our physical existence. This exploration of these physical-spiritual connections and body centered practices led to the creation of Hatha Yoga.

In the late 1800s and early 1900s yoga masters began to travel to the west, attracting attention and followers. In the 1920s Hatha Yoga was strongly promoted in India with the lifelong work of T. Krishnamacharya. Krishnamacharya travelled through India giving demonstrations of yoga poses and opened the first Hatha Yoga school. He produced three students that would continue his legacy and increase the popularity of Hatha Yoga, B.K.S. Iyengar , T.K.V. Desikachar and Pattabhi Jois.

The importation of yoga in the west continued slowly until the well known Indra Devi opened her yoga studio in Hollywood in 1947. Since then, many more western and Indian teachers have become pioneers, popularizing Hatha Yoga and gaining millions of followers. Hatha Yoga now has many different schools or styles, all emphasizing the many different aspects of the practice. Hatha Yoga or the Yoga of Postures is the aspect of Yoga that most people are aware of today although there are other branches, some with the emphasis more on meditation and philosophy than physical postures.

Developing a strong, healthy and flexible body is just one aspect of this ancient science. Yogis revere the body because they realize that a weak and tired body can be a hindrance towards spiritual progress. By being mindful of their breathing while they practice the various postures they discipline their minds. By disciplining their minds they are able to abide by the principles which yoga stands for. First amongst these principles is 'Ahimsa', or peacefulness in thought, deed, and action not only to other human beings, but also to all living creatures, and most importantly to our own selves. Remember this when you want to push yourself into a new yoga posture, you will be able to do it over a period of time, just be easy on yourself.

Anyone can practice yoga. You don't need any special equipment, clothing, or lessons; all you need is the will to pursue a healthier and happier lifestyle. The yoga postures and Asanas exercise every part of your body. The stretching helps in toning and strengthening your muscles and joints, including your spine and your entire skeletal system. Yoga not only improves your body but also aids in keeping your glands, nerves and your other internal organs in radiant health. By releasing physical and mental tension, you will liberate vast resources of energy. The yogic breathing exercises known as Pranayama revitalize the body and help control the mind, leaving you calm and refreshed; combine this with the practice of positive thinking and meditation and the result will be increased clarity, mental power and concentration.

THE FIVE PRINCIPLES OF YOGA

Relaxation: By releasing the tension in the muscles and putting the whole body at rest, you revitalize your nervous system and achieve inner peace, making you feel relaxed and refreshed. This relaxed feeling is carried over into all your activities and helps you conserve your energy and let go of all worries and fears.

Exercise: This principle revolves around the idea that our physical body is meant to move and exercise. Proper exercise is achieved through the yoga postures or Asana which systematically works on all parts of the body. They stretch and tone the muscles and ligaments, enhance the flexibility of the spine and the joints, and improve circulation. The Asanas are designed to regulate the physical and physiological functions of the body. Practicing these yoga poses makes your body relaxed, gives you more strength and energy, and rejuvenates the various systems of the body. Each movement and stretch should be guided by your breath, your movement and your breath should be coordinated and feel like one. The execution of the Asana is beneficial to the body, and at the same time contributes to spiritual and mental growth.

Breathing: This means breathing fully and rhythmically, making use of all the parts of your lungs to increase your oxygen intake. Proper breathing should be deep, slow and rhythmical. To achieve this, you need to be able to regulate the length and duration of your inhalation, exhalation, and the retention of air in your lungs or the pauses between breath. Yoga breathing exercises or Pranayama teach how you can recharge your body and control your mental state by regulating the flow of Prana - the life force. This helps you achieve a calmer and more focused mind, and increases your energy level.

Diet: What you eat deeply affects your mind. Poor diet results in mental inefficiency and blocks spiritual awareness. A good diet is one that nourishes both mind and body, it should be well balanced and based on natural foods. Proper diet in yoga also means eating in moderation and eating only when you are hungry. We sometimes tend to eat when we are upset, using food to fill the gap or the emptiness that we feel. Bad eating habits will cause our senses to be dull and we won't even notice how much we eat or how it tastes. Food should sustain our body, it should keep the body light and supple, the mind calm, and it should also help in keeping a strong immune system.

Meditation: The way we think highly affects our way of life. Practice keeping a positive outlook in life, this will encourage a peaceful mind. Positive thinking and meditation helps you remove negative thoughts and brings your mind under control.

BEGINNING A YOGA SESSION

One of the advantages of yoga is that it can be practiced almost anywhere, without special equipment, and by people of all ages. In looking for a place to practice, choose somewhere that is relatively free from distractions, the place should be quiet, clean and well ventilated. Using a mat, a blanket, or towel will provide support and added comfort when you do lying or sitting positions. It is best to wear loose or stretch clothing. Yoga is traditionally practiced barefoot; however socks or soft-shoes can be used. It is also best to practice yoga on an empty stomach or about one or two hours after a full meal. Go to the toilet if you need to, clean your nostrils and throat, and consume a glass of warm water 15 minutes before you start. You may eat fruit, an energy bar or drink a glass of juice or water an hour before to avoid getting really hungry during practice.

Practicing first thing in the morning is an excellent way to revitalize the mind and body. Yoga breathing and meditation at night helps induce a deep, restful sleep. Always start with easy poses to condition your body for the more difficult exercises that follow. Do not strain yourself, pause when you feel pain or fatigue and relaxing between difficult exercises is also beneficial. Yoga sessions need not be lengthy, but should be done daily. As little as 15 minutes of exercises and 10 minutes of breathing and meditation each day can yield benefits.

Here is a good routine for a basic yoga session:

- Warm-up Exercises - conditions your body for safe transition into Asana practice. For beginners, you may just use the warm-up poses (shown on the following pages) as your entire practice. Warm-up exercises 'open' the shoulder muscles, the spine, the hips, the lower back, and the groin.

- Standing Poses - for alignment of the feet and the body. Opens the hips, stretches the legs, strengthens your back and increases your range of movement. Standing poses facilitate digestion, blood circulation and are good for those who want to lose weight.

- Sitting Poses - sitting poses allow you to infuse the breath and prana, and to revitalize by giving you a calm and quiet feeling. These poses greatly contribute in shaping your buttocks and legs, and in adding vitality and suppleness to the spine.

- Twists - twist exercises release the tension in your spine, relieve backaches and make your shoulders more flexible. It also facilitates the circulation of blood and nutrients in the body.

- Supine and Prone Poses - these poses release tension in your abdomen and increase the mobility of your spine. They restore strength in your back, arms and legs, and release tension in your hips and groin.

- Inverted and Balance Poses - inverted and balance poses defy gravity and develop coordination, increase stamina and strength, and improve grace, agility and poise. They also improve your concentration and ability to focus.

- Backbends - backbends are the poses that benefit the adrenal glands and the kidney. They also release tension in your shoulders and pelvis, and improve the flexibility of your spine.

- Finishing Poses - these are the cooling-down exercises.

When performing the Asanas, try to concentrate on each movement - the process of moving is just as important as attaining a given position. Remember that you should not strain or continue holding any yoga posture if it causes pain. Yoga isn't a competitive sport, and the extent of the stretch is less important than the technique. Each Asana may be repeated up to three times, but it is better to perform a posture once correctly than repeating it three times quickly and sloppily. Try to perform the poses in the prescribed order, since the routine is meant to help balance the different muscle groups. Remember that yoga poses are done slowly and meditatively combined with abdominal breathing. These gentle movements not only reawaken your awareness and control of your body, but also have a profound effect spiritually, freeing you from fears and helping to instil confidence and serenity.

The following series of yoga poses is a great introduction to yoga routine. Make sure you follow the advice already given and don't push yourself too far. If you experience any pain stop immediately.

THE BOW

To begin lie face down on the ground with the knees bent and then raised in the direction of the head. Hold the ankles and, while inhaling, a pull should be exerted on the ankles so that the chest, head and thighs are raised up away from the floor. To start with it will not be possible to hold the legs together, but this will gradually occur with regular practice. This position should be maintained for up to ten breaths. To complete the bow, exhale and let go of the legs.

THE BRIDGE

Lie on your back, the knees should be bent, with the legs separated a little and the arms at the side of the body. Inhale and lift the torso and legs, thus forming a bridge. The fingers should then be linked under the body and the arms held straight. Then incline the body to each side in turn, ensuring that the shoulders stay underneath. To make the bridge a little bigger, pressure can be exerted by the arms and feet. After inhaling, the position should be maintained for a minimum of one minute and the body returned to a relaxed normal position on the floor.

THE SPINAL TWIST

Sit on the floor with legs outstretched. The left leg should be bent and placed over the other leg as far as possible. Exhale and twist the body to the left. The right hand should be moved towards the right foot. The body should be supported by placing the left hand on the ground at the back but keeping the back straight. Every time you exhale the body should be further twisted to the left. The position should be maintained for approximately one minute and then the complete action done again, but this time turning to the right. This is a gentle posture that is easy to perform. Relax. The spinal twist helps to strengthen the spine, improve posture and promote psychological balance.

THE TRIANGLE

Stand upright with the legs apart and the arms held out at shoulder level. Extend the right foot to the side and, upon exhaling, bend over the right-hand side so that the right hand slips downwards in the direction of the ankle. There should be no forward inclination of the body at this time. As the bending action takes place, the left arm should be lifted upright with the palm of the hand to the front. This stretched position should be kept up for the minimum of a minute, trying to extend the stretch as you exhale.

After inhaling, revert to the beginning of the exercise and do it again but leaning in the opposite direction. The triangle helps to calm the nerves, acts to remove toxins from the body, and promotes good health in general.

THE CAT

Begin by kneeling on all fours with your hands shoulder-distance apart

and your knees the same distance apart as your hands. Your elbows should remain straight throughout the entire exercise.

Exhale while arching your back up high. Keep your head between your arms, looking at your abdomen. Hold this pose for a few seconds. Inhale, as you slowly hollow your back to a concave position. Raise your head and look up. Hold again. Repeat the sequence five to ten times, creating a slow flowing movement of the two postures. Relax. The cat helps to strengthen the spine, improve posture and revitalize the whole body.

THE TREE

Stand with both feet together, arms loosely by your side. Focus your eyes on an imaginary spot directly ahead of you. Bring the right foot up and place the sole against the inside of the left thigh, as high as possible. When balanced, raise both arms simultaneously, placing the palms together over your head. Hold for 30 seconds. Gently lower your arms. Release your foot from your thigh. Repeat the sequence with the other foot. Relax. The tree promotes concentration, balance and stability of body and mind.

THE COBRA

Lie on your front and place the palms on the floor under the shoulders, fingers turned slightly inwards. Slowly lift the forehead, the nose, the chin, and the entire upper body, up to the navel. The weight rests on both hands, the pelvis, and the legs. Keep the elbows slightly bent, and do not allow the shoulders to hunch up towards the ears. Hold for ten seconds, focusing your attention on the lower back. Very slowly lower your trunk to the floor, then the chin, the nose, and the forehead and relax. The cobra increases blood supply to the abdominal organs and helps to relieve digestive problems and correct kidney malfunctions.

THE PLOUGH

Lie on the floor and slowly raise your legs and trunk off the floor. Supporting your hips with both hands, bring your legs slightly over your head. Keep your legs as straight as possible. Supporting your back with both hands, continue lifting your legs up and over your head until the toes come to rest on the floor behind your head. Only when you are quite comfortable in the position, release the hold on your back and place your arms flat on the floor. Hold only for ten seconds in the beginning. After your body becomes accustomed to this position, you may hold it longer. Very slowly unroll your body to the starting position. Relax. The plough helps to reinvigorate the entire nervous system, removing fatigue, listlessness and exhaustion. It is of particular benefit to the pancreas and endocrine glands.

THE FORWARD BEND

Sit with your legs stretched out in front of you, knees very straight. Inhale and stretch your arms above your head. Exhale and very slowly and smoothly bend forward from the hips *(not from the waist)* to grasp your toes. If at first this seems difficult, clasp instead your ankles, calves, or knees. It is important that your legs remain straight. Continue to bend forward and down, aiming to touch your knees with your head. Hold for at least ten seconds and observe your breath. Release your hold and very slowly unroll your spine, returning to a sitting position. Repeat twice. The forward bend slows the respiratory rate to produce a calm and relaxed state of mind. It also increases the suppleness of the spine and improves blood circulation.

SALUTE (GREETING) TO THE SUN

These twelve positions have the aim of relaxing and invigorating the body and mind. This classic yoga exercise coordinates breathing with variations of six yoga poses in a flowing rhythmic way that stretches and relaxes your body and your mind. As suggested by its name, it was originally done when the sun rose and when it set. Although these stances are quite safe, they should not be done by pregnant women or those having a monthly period, except with expert tuition. If a person has hypertension (high blood pressure), a hernia, clots in the blood or pain in the lower back they are also not recommended. Each exercise should follow on smoothly one after the other.

1 Stand up as straight as you can without forcing it, with your feet

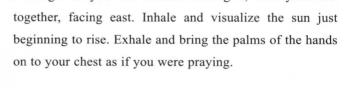

together, facing east. Inhale and visualize the sun just beginning to rise. Exhale and bring the palms of the hands on to your chest as if you were praying.

2 Inhale and stretch the arms upright with the palms facing the ceiling and lean backwards, pushing the pelvis forward a little, and look up at your hands.

3 Exhale and, keeping the legs straight, place the fingers or palms on to the ground, ideally, your hands are touching the floor in front of or beside your feet. (Don't force this, if you can't reach the floor, let your hands hold on to the lowest part of your legs they can reach.)

4 Inhale and bend the knees and place one leg straight out backwards, with the knee touching the ground, in a long, lunging movement. Turn your toes right under and straighten your body from head to heel.

5 With both hands on the ground, raise the head slightly and push the hips to the front. At the same time as holding the breath, stretch the legs out together backwards, and raise the body off the floor supported by the arms.

6 Exhale and fold the body over bent knees so that the head touches the ground with the arms stretched out in front, toes curled, until you are in the classic push-up position.

7 After inhaling and exhaling once, drop your knees to the floor, with your bottom up. Bend the elbows and bring your chest and chin to the floor. Continue breathing out and lower the whole body to the floor, straightening your legs and keeping your toes curled under with the body being supported by the hands at shoulder level and also by the toes. The stomach and hips should not be on the ground.

8 After taking a deep breath, stretch the arms and push the body upwards pushing down on your hands and slowly lifting your head as you straighten the elbows. Arch your back upwards like a snake before it strikes.

9 Exhale and then raise the hips upwards with the feet and hands being kept on the floor so that the body is in an inverted V-shape. The legs and back should be kept straight.

10 Breathe in and lunge forward by bending your right knee and stepping your right foot forward between your hands. When you breathe out, straighten your right leg and bring the left foot next to the right. Lift your buttocks high until you are touching your toes.

11 Inhale and slowly lift the spine, visualizing it unroll one vertebra at a time. Raise your head and look up, bringing your arms straight overhead, and bring the image of the rising sun back to mind.

12 Place the feet together keeping the legs straight. Breathe out and slowly bring your arms back to the sides, allowing the sun to glow brighter and brighter in your mind's eye.

Salute the sun six times at first, gradually increasing the number of repetitions, although if you do not have much time just a few can still feel great. It is suggested to alternate the leading leg used each time.

Yoga has recently been used to treat some illnesses such as rheumatoid arthritis, however if a person has such a severe disorder then a highly skilled and experienced therapist is essential. If you think yoga might aggravate your condition consult a yoga teacher before you begin.

Many thanks to www.abc-of-yoga.com and www.yogabasics.com for providing information for this chapter.

11
MEDITATION

There are many different types of meditation, most of them aim to relax the body and promote peaceful and positive states of mind. The benefits of regular meditation are now well known, we gain improved health and well being, more energy, levels of stress are greatly reduced and positive, peaceful and confident states of mind are easily generated. As healers or therapists if we have a little experience of the benefits of meditation we can share this with others by teaching clients, patients, friends or family how to relax the body and mind and generate a positive outlook. The beauty of teaching a patient a simple relaxation technique is that they can do this a little every day in between treatments, which will greatly assist their mental, emotional and physical healing.

Meditation is a very simple, natural and powerful way of realizing our abilities to become more whole, healthy and happy human beings from within. Meditation is not difficult and it does not take years, months or even weeks to master. We can receive great benefit even from our very first meditation session. To gain the most from meditation it can be really helpful to find a local meditation group that is lead by an experienced teacher, (See Appendix 1). However we can learn the basics if we follow the instructions carefully and gain great benefit from practicing for just 10-15 minutes per day.

RELAXATION MEDITATION

This can be done either sitting or lying down. Relaxing music may help and you will need fifteen or twenty minutes of free time. Although meditation relaxes the body and mind you shouldn't feel sleepy, in fact when you have finished you should feel refreshed, as if you have rested well. With this in mind you may find it more beneficial to meditate sitting in a chair in a quiet room without music, keeping the spine straight but relaxed helps to prevent feelings of sleepiness. You will find out through your own experience what works best for you.

Begin by making a conscious intention to completely relax your body and mind. Take some deep breaths and settle into a comfortable position. Try to let go of anything that might be on your mind; this is your time to relax properly and it is important that nothing distracts you.

Bring your attention to your toes and try to 'find' any tension and release it. At first it may be helpful to tense and then release them, we need to gradually familiarise ourselves with the experience of consciously relaxing, then the process will become easier. Move your attention slowly into the rest of your feet, consciously relaxing each part. If it helps you can think 'release and relax', then slowly bring your attention to the ankles, shins, calves, knees etc. Continue to gradually move your attention up through the body, consciously relaxing each part. If your attention wanders, simply return to where you were. When you have reached the top of your head spend a few minutes being aware of how it feels to be completely relaxed. The more we remember this experience the easier it will become to repeat and carry forward into our daily activities. This technique can take some time to master so don't be disappointed if you still feel some tension after the first few sessions, this will pass in time and the technique will become natural. At this point we can stop or we can continue with a simple visualisation.

HEALING VISUALISATION

Visualise a spiralling stream of golden or white light entering through the crown of your head and filling every part of your body; again try to move the light slowly down so you get a sensation that each part of your body and every cell is filled with 'light' energy. We can then imagine that our whole body and mind melts into this light which slowly expands to fill the room, the house, town and country, the whole planet and finally the whole of space. Then spend some time enjoying this experience of pure light filling the whole of space. If you are ill especially try to feel that your illness and all its symptoms have melted in to light. This visualisation can be very powerful and uplifting and especially helpful for those with constant health problems. We can combine this meditation with prayer by simply asking for healing before we begin or imagining/feeling that we are becoming closer to God or our spiritual nature as the meditation progresses.

We can take the meditation a step further by thinking of others who may need healing, local or world conflicts, disasters or simply 'every living being'. Visualise these people or situations surrounded by the light that has come from within you and imagine that all their problems or sickness are easily transformed and healed, then just continue to visualise them as healthy, happy and content for a few minutes. We can think, 'how wonderful, these people are now actually free from their pain and problems', try to really believe that this has actually happened. Then concentrate for as long as possible on the feeling of joy that arises from this thought.

Don't worry if at first this feels false or manufactured, with sincere, regular practice your motivation will become more natural and powerful. Also don't try too hard or make your visualisations too complicated, an honest intention and a strong belief that your positive thoughts have really helped is the most important aspect.

The power of the mind is limitless, by strongly imagining that through our actions people are released from their problems, this creates the causes for it to actually happen in the future, even though realistically our mind is quite limited at present! When you have finished, visualise the light coming slowly back into the space of your body and seal it in with a mental intention like:

'Balanced, centred, grounded, blessed and protected',

Then get up slowly when you are ready and mentally dedicate the positive energy you have created for some good purpose like world peace. When we do anything selfless or positive we create positive energy or good karma, this can be lost if we later lose our temper or get frustrated with someone or something! Dedicating our good energy to a greater cause like world peace seals and protects it and prevents us from damaging our own good work.

If you are teaching this kind of healing meditation to others you can adapt it to suit their own beliefs or background. Never give false hope by saying that this meditation can cure illness, it is probably better to say that it can help to relieve symptoms at best and if anything extra happens that is a bonus.

There are many types of healing meditation. In the Buddhist tradition there is the practice of the 'Medicine Buddha', the embodiment of the healing power of all enlightened beings. This involves a special kind of meditation, prayer, visualisation and receiving healing blessings which we can do for ourselves or for others who need healing. It is also possible to receive a Medicine Buddha empowerment this helps us to develop a close connection with this healing Buddha and makes this healing practice more powerful. If you want to know more about this look for a Buddhist Centre near you, see Appendix 1.

MEDITATION FOR DEVELOPING COMPASSION

There are many benefits to this kind of meditation, we become a clear channel for healing energy, we can purify some of our own negative karma and we gradually become a much happier person! This meditation has the power to completely solve most of our everyday problems. Since most of our problems come from thinking and feeling that we are the most important person on the planet by developing a deeper empathy and awareness of others we naturally begin to let go of our own sense of self importance. Our own problems become less important and eventually disappear in to a new sense of inner peace which naturally comes from our increasing love for others. In short, less 'self' and more 'others', in a balanced way, makes for a happy life and swift spiritual progress.

We prepare for this type of meditation by finding a regular daily quiet time, about fifteen to twenty minutes or more if we wish; early morning is often best when we are fresh and this can really help us start and continue the day in a positive way. The room we use should be peaceful and clean and if we have a particular religious belief we can set up a small shrine or altar with holy pictures, scriptures and offerings. This serves as a spiritual focal point and helps to build and hold a good quality of energy in the room and makes it a space conducive to meditation.

As mentioned it is better to meditate sitting in a chair with our back straight but not tense, our feet flat on the floor and hands resting in our lap, or we can sit on a floor cushion in a traditional meditation posture.

Again we can relax the body and focus the mind by mentally scanning the body for tension and releasing it; we begin at the top of the head and slowly work down through the various parts of the body until we reach the toes.

Then we bring our attention to our breathing and particularly to the sensation at the tip of the nostrils as we feel the cool air coming in and the warm air as we breathe out. Focus on this one sensation completely; our breathing is the 'object' of meditation. This focuses the mind and improves our clarity and concentration, in fact this simple breathing meditation, if practised for ten or fifteen minutes daily, can greatly improve our quality of life by giving us a clear and peaceful mind.

If we 'lose' our object of meditation and begin thinking about other things, then when we realise this we simply bring our attention back to the sensation of the breath in the nostrils. This process of losing and 'finding' the object of meditation will happen many times before our concentration becomes more focussed and stable. Sometimes it may take weeks before our mind starts to relax and accept its new master! So keep trying and don't expect too much too soon. If we have no experience of meditation it can be helpful to practice breathing meditation for several days or weeks before trying anything else. Once our mind is relaxed and focussed we can begin the next part of the meditation.

There are two parts to the next stage of this meditation; these are Contemplation and Placement. Contemplation is the mental process of considering the benefits of abandoning negative thoughts and actions and adopting positive ones. When as a result of this reasoning a strong wish arises in the mind to change our behaviour for the better, then this is our object of Placement and we 'hold-it' or experience it for as long as possible.

To develop compassion we can go straight to the main part of the meditation explained in the next paragraph or we can first contemplate how the opposite of compassion, anger, causes so many problems. The selfish mind of anger is responsible for all conflicts, wars and relationship problems, without anger we would live in a very peaceful world. Also contemplate how angry or selfish thoughts and feelings cause many personal problems and great unhappiness and consider how wonderful it would be to be free from these heavy negative minds. When we naturally feel a strong wish to let go of anger in our life try to hold that wish for as long as possible, if you forget it return to the contemplation until it arises again.

Then after a few minutes begin to contemplate the problems that others experience in their lives. We can think about people we know who are very unhappy or we can think about situations we have heard about or seen on TV where people or animals are suffering. When a feeling of compassion arises in the mind towards others we hold on to it for as long as possible and try to mix our mind with it completely, almost as if we have become compassion. Compassion in this context is a wish for others to be free from suffering, it is not sadness or pity or sorrow although these emotions often precede it. This wish is our main object of meditation; it is a very transforming, powerful and positive mind. At the end of our meditation session we can make a firm determination to help others whenever we can and try to remember that determination throughout the rest of the day.

We should come out of meditation feeling that we have changed, at least a little. We should feel relaxed, clear and empowered with positive energy, our mind should feel expanded, more aware of others and less focussed on our own small world. Again this may not happen at first, it may take weeks or even months to really understand the process of meditation from our own direct experience. But if we keep trying of course we will definitely improve and the benefits we feel will continually increase.

Try to keep your meditations simple and powerful, remember that you are just using your intellect to generate a powerful feeling of love or compassion and then hold that feeling for as long as possible. If your mind wanders simply return to the contemplation until that strong wish for others to be free from suffering arises, then again gently but firmly focus on that determination for as long as possible.

When we 'hold' or focus on an object of meditation we should not strain the mind, it should feel natural, as if our mind has completely mixed or become 'one' with the object of meditation i.e. our wish to be more tolerant, patient or compassionate. With meditation we are actually training ourselves to eventually think and feel this way quite naturally. Although it might feel quite unnatural at first, by regularly developing these deep wishes to change for the better we will definitely become more positive, happy, content and considerate. This ancient tried and tested way of dealing with life's problems, if practised correctly and regularly, is a guaranteed solution and unlike other modern methods of finding happiness, addiction to it produces very healthy results!

Our meditations will be more powerful if they are based on our own life experience and personal observations of the world around us. There is no point meditating every day on a vague wish to love others if in our hearts we are not really interested in changing. We have to mentally make the meditations come alive and then carry our good intentions forward into the rest of the day. We do this by remembering the positive feelings and determination that arose during our meditation and use these to guide all our thoughts and actions throughout the day. Whenever we become aware that negative feelings or thoughts, like worry or impatience, are about to arise in the mind we can prevent them influencing us by recalling our earlier good intentions. In this way our wisdom and happiness will gradually increase and our daily problems will steadily decrease.

One of the special qualities of authentic meditation is that it increases our wisdom. Wisdom is simply the ability to understand clearly where lasting happiness comes from. As we meditate daily we will come to see that happiness is simply a state of mind and that since we have the opportunity to create positive states of mind through meditation, prayer and so on, these methods are the key to lasting happiness.

Although the essence and practice of meditation is quite simple as mentioned it is a good idea to seek out a fully qualified and experienced teacher who can guide us along the stages of the path of meditation. Learning and sharing our experiences with others, meditating in a group and having the opportunity to ask questions can greatly assist our enjoyment and progress. Also having a teacher who is a living example of what we can achieve through meditation is a constant inspiration and encouragement to our own developing practice. If you want to find a Meditation group in your area see Appendix 1. If we do a little meditation every day the good results will accumulate, we shall become more relaxed and more able to enjoy life fully and gradually we shall become a true source of wisdom, compassion and inner strength for others.

12
GOOD HEALING PRACTICE

The main objective of any healing technique is to restore inner and outer health as quickly and easily as possible. It would be wonderful if that could happen every time, however we do not live in a perfect world so our aims have to be realistically adjusted to reflect what can be practically achieved. Sometimes we may only achieve a reduction in the severity of the symptoms and this improvement might have to be maintained with regular treatments. However we can regard such a treatment as successful if we or the patient are happy with such improvements. The patient's attitude to their condition is of paramount importance. Encouraging positive mental and emotional qualities through using a combination of healing techniques combined with good listening and good advice is the best way we can help. A positive mind is a wonderful bi-product of any good healing technique and one of the most important factors in the healing process. We can even verify the power of a positive mind on health through the results of scientific research, it's official being happy is good for you!

In fact restoring a good mental attitude should be our number one priority. There are many people in this world who have to deal with severe suffering of one form or another yet many do so with a happy mind, a contented mind, a mind that wishes no more than that very happiness. Are such people healthy, do they need healing? In Tibet it was not unusual for highly experienced meditators to pray for difficult conditions and situations that they could use to develop an even stronger mind!

If we are embarking on a journey towards an understanding of the 'way of healing' then from the start we need to develop a little wisdom to temper and shape the power of our compassionate wish to help others. Wisdom is essential. We can be the most technically accomplished and compassionate healer but without a little simple wisdom many of our actions can be misguided and our time and effort wasted. Strange as it may seem good physical health might not always be the healer's main concern. If you want to learn a little more about this special way of life read 'Everything is a Blessing' by David Vennels (O Books).

PROFESSIONAL PRACTICE

If you wish to practice any of the techniques explained in this book on a professional level, you will need to pursue a recognised course of study and obtain the relevant qualifications. This is as much for your own benefit as for the people you will be treating. You will need to obtain professional indemnity insurance and again you will need a recognised qualification for this. There are many courses available today, if you cannot find a college try contacting the relevant professional body; they should be able to help you. The courses are not difficult and generally very interesting, enjoyable and well structured so that anyone can complete them with confidence in their ability to treat others. You will also meet many people of like mind and benefit from the company and sharing of ideas about your chosen therapy.

With all the techniques explained in this book you can start practicing the basic techniques straight away. You can do no damage and the more 'hands on' experience you get the better you will become, although again you should only practice on those you know well, until you feel fully competent, and never make any claims that you can cure any kind of illness. When friends and family experience the pleasure and positive results of a good treatment then you will have a long queue of willing patients beating a path to your door! Learning these healing techniques can be the beginning of a fascinating and mind expanding new phase in your life and when you begin to get good results this can really encourage you to learn more and hone your skills to perfection. There will be a real sense of accomplishment and satisfaction in seeing the benefits others derive from your skills.

PREPARING FOR TREATMENT

If you are treating someone for the first time put yourself in their position, how did you feel when you first received any form of complementary treatment? Try to make them as welcome and comfortable as possible, without being overbearing. Give them time to explain why they have come to see you and what they hope to gain from the treatment, i.e. their 'intentions'. Give yourself a suitable period of uninterrupted time, you might need about 50 minutes depending on which therapy you are using and on your experience and the patient's requirements. Try to avoid potential distractions by using an answer phone, not answering the front door and asking others not to disturb you during the treatment. It can also be useful to have a clock within view to keep track of time. Some people are physically and mentally energised by these healing techniques and others are left feeling relaxed and ready to unwind, so be aware of this and don't take either as a good or a bad sign as the good results of a treatment can take days to become apparent. You may need a quiet, warm, peaceful and clean environment in which to work. Of course if you are working from other people's homes you will have to adapt accordingly. However you can warn them beforehand that the treatment will be more effective if the room that you use is at least warm and quiet and that you will not be disturbed.

If you have access to a treatment/interview room there are lots of things you can do to make it feel really peaceful and welcoming. Some obvious pointers are the décor, subtle colours and pleasant pictures are effective along with flowers, plants and one or two comfy chairs to be used when you are talking to the client before and after the treatment. Also crystals, aromatherapy burners and appropriate relaxing music all go to create the right conditions conducive to successful treatments. However, despite the best preparations if we do not know how to treat our client/patient with respect, empathy, wisdom and understanding then we are fighting a losing battle. If the patient has confidence and faith in your abilities and feels relaxed and able to talk freely without fear of judgement then you can be assured that the barriers to healing will be gradually worn down.

FIRST TREATMENT

You may need to explain exactly what the treatment is, how it works and what it entails, so think about how you will do this. There is no reason to overload people with details but it can be helpful to explain the basics and it gives people confidence in your abilities if you obviously know what you are talking about. Also on the first appointment you will have to ask the person you are treating to read and sign a disclaimer, although this is mainly only important if you are practicing professionally. Again such topics will be covered on a practitioners' training course together with taking case notes and the client's personal details and medical history.

So if you are treating someone for the first time it may be helpful to tell them what to expect during a treatment. However judge every situation as you think best, sometimes it may not seem appropriate as the patient may then be thinking about what might happen instead of just relaxing. Here are some examples of what you may wish to tell them if you are using a mainly physical therapy and if it feels like the right thing to do:

- How long the treatment takes, how you will cover the body, if relevant, and that they will remain mainly covered throughout the treatment
- Demonstrate the basic techniques and let them know that they can just relax and switch off
- They may experience warmth in and around the body and/or coming from your hands, occasionally it may feel cool instead!
- Also tingling sensations may be felt in and around the body
- A sense of heaviness or lightness
- They may feel very relaxed or even sleepy
- They may want to talk, which is fine
- Their body may sweat slightly or twitch sometimes and they may feel some 'movement' within the body as they relax
- Their stomach may 'gurgle' as their body relaxes
- Also their throat may become dry, so have a glass of water at hand, and tissues for a 'runny' nose!

Explain that these are all natural reactions. Some people may have much deeper and more profound experiences and/or emotional releases, so again a box of tissues and of course an ability to listen may be useful. Try to be open and accept whatever arises and trust that the client will know consciously or subconsciously what they are ready to release and/or deal with. The more genuine trust and confidence we have in others' natural healing abilities the easier it will be for those qualities to naturally arise within them. From the practitioner's side, developing this trust in the process of natural healing is part of our own healing and growth, it also creates the right atmosphere and conditions conducive to 'ripening' the clients own self-healing potential.

It is important to have a relaxed state of mind and to enjoy your work. There is not much point in treating others when we have a negative, impatient, bored or inattentive attitude. It will show in your work, people will notice and lose confidence in you and the treatment. In fact, if we can strive to develop a relaxed, peaceful and compassionate state of mind then this will greatly assist the effectiveness of the treatment. We may think that this is impossible; how can a state of mind positively affect an apparently physical therapy? Well, we can look at this is different ways. Certainly if we went to see a therapist who had an impatient and condescending attitude this would make us feel uncomfortable and alternatively when we are in the company of people who are deeply peaceful and caring we naturally feel some benefits from their presence. Also many people believe that the healer is also acting as a channel for healing energy and that touch can act as a kind of energetic gateway for the patient to receive this. Definitely some people have a natural ability to heal others simply through touch and it is often those that are attracted to the healing professions that possess such latent healing potential. To successfully channel such healing energy from wherever we believe it comes from we need a peaceful, relaxed mind, a feeling of compassion or empathy for our patient and a wish for them to receive whatever they need without grasping at success or being worried about failure in this regard. If we have a religion then faith is very important and we can always say silent prayers for our patient before each treatment and ask for guidance, blessings and healing inspiration. Again if we do not see regular miracles we should not be surprised, disappointed or discouraged. We do not know what people really need in their lives. It is difficult for us to see the 'big picture' and sometimes there is a lot to be gained from having to develop the inner resources to live with a challenging illness. If we can impart this information skilfully and at the right time then we may be doing our client a greater favour than if we were to simply take away their illness or disability.

Give the patient time to talk and collect themselves after the treatment and have a drink and a biscuit handy as a little sugar and liquid can help people become 'grounded' and alert after a very relaxing treatment. This is especially important if they have to drive home. If you are doing several successive treatments give yourself a few minutes rest between each treatment and set a mental intention to relax and recharge yourself. Don't take on too much too soon. In the beginning just do a few treatments per week. This will give you time to build up your strength, stamina and concentration. If you find that you are drained after a treatment, are you too tense during the treatment or are you using too much pressure? We are not forcing the patient to get better, just gently encouraging good health to arise.

HOW MANY TREATMENTS?

Whatever therapy or combination of therapies we are using we can usually tell after the first three or four treatments if the condition we are treating is going to respond favourably. It is really up to the patient to decide how long they wish to continue regular treatment. As mentioned, over-stimulating a body that is already overtaxed with a serious illness can cause more problems. The answer is 'gently does it'.

Some people may not need any follow-up treatments after the initial 6 or 8 weeks and some people may want to continue every week, or something in between may be more suitable, like once per month. We are not only there to help cure and relieve sickness and disease but to also act as a form of life enhancing and revitalising therapist so we need to be imaginative and really take a deep interest in the patient's lifestyle and state of mind. We should try to work out a healing plan which can involve healing techniques, a change of diet, homeopathic or herbal remedies and some self help techniques like meditation. We need to combine therapies, techniques and good advice that are best for the individual given their current physical condition and capacity for inner and outer change. Correct combining is a skill that needs to be developed over time and the only way to develop this is through lots of hands-on practical experience.

When treating children their attention span and hence their ability to lie still for a full physical treatment may be limited. So we can give them shorter, more frequent treatments. Obviously if we do not know the child well a parent or guardian must be present throughout the treatment. It's not surprising that children are usually more naturally understanding and intuitively wise to natural healing techniques, consequently this trust and openness often brings swifter results.

TYPICAL REACTIONS

Typical reactions during and after a physical body treatment are:

- increased energy
- inner peace and a feeling of warmth within and/or around the body
- gentle tingling sensations

- a sense of energy flowing in and/or around the body
- clearer senses
- lessening of stress and emotional problems
- improved physical health
- increased ability to deal positively with stressful situations
- increased clarity of mind and deeper intuitive or inner wisdom
- a sense of 'coming home' and of being in touch with 'the flow' of life
- deepening of spiritual awareness and experiences e.g. seeing or sensing auras, energy, colours etc
- a general feeling of being more whole, healthy and happy, a more complete sense of self

Everyone is different, some people may feel nothing during a treatment and this is also normal! Physical therapies work in the way that we need it as individuals so we should not expect any two people to react in the same way, even when they have the same illness.

Occasionally a 'cleansing' period of body and mind may occur after the first few treatments this might be especially true if the patient has a serious illness. This might involve:

- a short minor illness i.e. cold, flu
- sweating
- headaches
- frequent urination
- a need to sleep more,
- a need to drink more
- temporary loss or increase in appetite

- some other minor physical problems, some type of emotional release i.e. crying, laughing

These symptoms are a positive sign that the patient's body is working well to heal itself and we can encourage the client by telling them this. However, it is not a definite sign that they will regain health so as always be careful what you say. If symptoms of detox are persistent and severe reduce the regularity of treatments and/or remedies. Again encouraging the patient to drink plenty of clear water, perhaps even three or four pints a day, can also help.

It is quite common for people to feel tired or sleepy for days after a treatment, this is a good sign that they are beginning to learn how to finally 'open' and fully relax. Often the amount of stress we carry goes unnoticed as we move from one thing in life to another. The habit of stress and the layers of stress gradually accumulate in our system, both physically and mentally, to the extent that we never allow ourselves time to just 'be' who we are. We can even build up and carry stress with us from one lifetime to another for many lifetimes. This accumulated stress acts as a barrier to healing, inner peace and a sense of our timeless spirituality, to the extent that we forget our true nature as primarily spiritual beings. Practising natural healing techniques, meditation, prayer or deep relaxation is a way to gradually release stress, cleanse the body/mind and re-introduce us to ourselves.

Learning to deeply relax, open our mind and allow stress, often in the form of negative thought patterns, to arise from within and fall away can sometimes be unnerving, as we often feel these aspects of our mind are part of our own sense of self or true identity. So this process can sometimes leave us feeling a little 'naked' and unsure of ourselves.

However, given time and a little positive experience we will develop the confidence and wish to consciously seek and appreciate this inner path towards a more whole and healthy way of living/being.

HELPING THE HEALING PROCESS

There are some obvious but very important things that we can do to help the natural healing process in ourselves and we can also give this advice to others. These suggestions are not essential and not everyone would find them helpful so only suggest them to patients if you think they are appropriate:

- Eat healthily, a well balanced diet including lots of fresh fruit and vegetables
- Cut down on alcohol
- Cut down on smoking or stop altogether if you can
- Avoid caffeine drinks and try to drink lots of still mineral water or herbal teas
- Cut down on chocolate, sweets or other refined foods
- Try to eat only fresh food products and perhaps consider a short water or juice fast but only if you have experience of fasting
- Avoid confrontational or stressful situations, try to keep a peaceful, happy and relaxed mind
- Spend some quiet time on your own in a peaceful place, go for walks in pleasant surroundings
- Meditate or pray for 10-20 minutes each day or simply spend this time in silence or reading a spiritual text
- Think positively! Essentially try to approach life with a relaxed, positive and open mind

The effects of following these simple guidelines can be quite dramatic. If we ask our patients to set a target to follow them all for seven days, or even better three weeks, they will see that it makes a big difference to their state of well being. These physical and mental benefits can really inspire them to continue for longer periods until they become regular habits. They are sowing the seeds for good health now and in the future.

If you think there maybe a serious undetected physical problem try not to alarm your client but do encourage them to see their own doctor, especially if they also feel something is not 'right'. They can always ask and should never be afraid to see another doctor for a second opinion about their current medical condition. If you are a professional complementary therapist all your clients who are seeking help for serious medical complaints should come to you after or whilst they are being treated by their own doctor.

BECOMING A GOOD HEALER

The client/therapist relationship is of paramount importance. Obviously any patient would be put off by an overbearing, self-important and 'loud' therapist. These qualities would leave the patient in doubt about the ability of the practitioner and the effectiveness of the therapist. Conversely if the therapist is quietly confident, kind, considerate, patient and willing to listen then this immediately instils confidence and a certain amount of faith and encouragement in the patient. As therapists we need to be in a frame of mind that allows the patient to feel comfortable and at ease with us. Really we need to be at a place in our own mental and spiritual evolution where we have developed certain qualities that allow us to be a catalyst for healing.

This may sound a little mystical but it is a truth. If we are shallow, materialistic, self-centered and in it for the money, praise or recognition then we really have nothing to give. How do we develop the special qualities that will transform us into an effective therapist? The first step is to steadily and continuously develop the wish to be such a person and much of the rest is simply learning from our life experiences and interpreting them with wisdom. Following a recognised path of spiritual and personal growth can be very helpful as part of this process.

In everyday life we meet some people that we feel 'uncomfortable' with and some that we just don't like! If you are faced with this situation with a patient, not liking them will not affect the quality of the physical treatment but will obviously affect the quality of the client/therapist relationship. In these situations try to be like a good doctor and develop a warm and friendly professional relationship equally with all your 'patients', without being particularly attached to some or averse to others. Another strategy is to use the situation to discover more about yourself. Think 'why do I not like this person, what is this situation telling me about myself?' Often the people and situations that we find difficult to deal with are reflections of some part of our own mind that we do not fully 'own' or understand, like a missing piece of the jigsaw.

This also applies to situations or people we are deeply attached to or depend upon for our happiness and peace of mind. Most of our relationships are tainted with aspects of 'need' or aversion, often we need the approval or simply the presence of others to feel secure, happy and whole and it easy to think of many things we dislike or disapprove of in others. We don't have to be completely self sufficient and separate or completely reliant on others for our wellbeing, there is a middle way. We can learn to give and receive without needing others to feel whole or pushing others away to feel 'free'. This way of living leads to meaningful relationships and a sense of personal freedom. This feeling of equanimity is also a good attribute to develop and apply to all areas of our lives. If we try to cultivate a balanced, warm and friendly attitude towards everyone we meet all our relationships will be naturally harmonious.

On the whole, given the right conditions, everyone has the natural ability to heal himself or herself. In some ways being a therapist gives us the ability to provide these healing conditions, when others cannot initially help themselves. The less we interfere with this process the better. Too much good intentioned advice can confuse people who may be already trying to deal with a difficult illness and changes in lifestyle. We don't always know what is best for others! Often we want to give what others do not need and trying to provide answers for others can definitely lessen their ability to resolve their own issues.

The 'good' healer to some extent steps back from being a 'solver of problems' and becomes more of an 'enabler' or simply a healing witness. This allows people to draw through the healer, and from within themselves, what they actually need to help them overcome or transform their own situation either physically, mentally or emotionally. This 'sustainable healing' allows people to develop the qualities that either consciously or subconsciously they need to help themselves. It also provides them with the skills they may need to deal with similar problems in the future. This can be a slow process at first, but gradually healing the inner problems lays the foundations for a deep and lasting overall healing that is more than worth a little extra time and effort.

If we seem to be attracting people with similar problems this is an indication that we may need to move forward in those areas as well, there is usually a strong connection between the problems people bring to us as healers and our own 'issues'. We can't expect other people to change for the better if we are not prepared to be honest about and challenge our own shortcomings! We don't have to be perfect, just prepared to learn more about ourselves. We should never feel pride about being a healer or act in a superior way, this can be a real barrier to our own healing and to improving our own healing abilities. If we try to be honest about our weaknesses, without being hard on ourselves and if we are able to share our problems and ask for help when we need it, then our own ability to heal ourselves and others will continue

REALISTIC EXPECTATIONS

The cause of all illness has its root in the mind and therein also lies the cure of all illness. If the mind is not ready or willing to change on an obvious or subtle level, the illness will not be cured, or we may only achieve temporary relief. It appears that everyone has the wish to be healthy, however very few people know themselves well enough to recognise that their illness is an expression of some part of their own mind that does not wish to be healthy or that does not know how to be well. We can re-teach ourselves to be well if we are willing to be patient and look within for the answers and not hand over the responsibility for our health to others. Healing works on all levels but principally on a mental and emotional level first, so don't be surprised if a physical condition does not disappear overnight. Good healing techniques work to achieve long term improvements by helping the person address, heal and release the issues that initially caused the problem and this may happen obviously or in a very subtle way. Sometimes just learning to accept and live with a major illness is all we can help people achieve, depending on the severity and duration of the problem. We should never regard this as failure, if their quality of life has improved only a little we should be pleased with this progress.

GOOD INTENTIONS

To make our healing actions more powerful and meaningful there are two simple things we can do. If we are preparing to practice any kind of physical therapy or before meeting a patient we can begin with a short prayer, affirmation or mental 'intention' and finish with a brief 'dedication'. Intention is everything! Our intention is what creates our 'karma'. Although this is explained in more detail later, briefly, everything we do, say and think, every action of body, speech and mind creates a potential in the mind for a corresponding physical, verbal or mental reaction in the future. It also creates the habit or tendency for us to repeat such actions in the future and an increased wish or compulsion to keep performing similar actions. If we perform negative actions we can expect negative re-actions sooner or later.

Also if we generally have a negative approach to life we are more likely to create the conditions that attract problems and difficult circumstances. Likewise the positive energy we create by developing, patience, kindness or giving healing will return to us as a very positive experience in one form or another. If we set a very positive mental intention before we perform any type of healing action or indeed any form of giving or beneficial action, then this will greatly increase the power of our karma. If this intention is wise and heart felt the consequences of our actions can benefit countless living beings, although we cannot directly see this incredible result. Basically if our motivation is to benefit others rather than ourselves then this will create very powerful and positive karma. To set an intention we just need to sit quietly for a few minutes, calm the mind and think of those people we would like to benefit. Then we can simply think or pray:

'Through the force of these healing actions may (name the people you are thinking of) find lasting happiness and good health'.

Or even more powerfully:

'May all living beings gain lasting benefit from these healing actions'.

When the treatment is over we can dedicate our positive actions or good karma. Dedication is similar to intention. If we consciously 'dedicate' or direct this positive energy for a specific purpose, this can be a very powerful way of manifesting our intentions, achieving our goals and accelerating our spiritual or personal growth. Whenever we create positive energy by helping others in any way or by consciously developing positive states of mind, we can dedicate this energy.

Choosing a purpose or direction for dedication is similar to creating an intention. If we can choose a purpose that will benefit many people then this wish will be fulfilled more easily than a purely selfish purpose. To dedicate after any positive action we can simply think or pray:

'May this positive energy be fully dedicated for the greatest good of all living beings' Or

'May every living being benefit from these positive actions'.

Perhaps the greatest goals we could wish for are:

'Through the force of these positive actions may every living being be released from suffering and may we all find true lasting happiness swiftly and easily', and/or

'Through the force of these positive actions may my wisdom and compassion continually increase for the benefit of others'.

This mental practice only takes a short time but this small gesture is a very special practice. We can easily waste or destroy the potential of previous positive actions or good karma simply by developing negative states of mind like anger, guilt or jealousy. <u>Sincere</u> and heartfelt dedication is like 'banking' or protecting the potential of our positive actions for our own and others' future benefit. In this way the potential of our good thoughts, words and deeds can only increase and will produce excellent results for ourselves and everyone in the future.

13

A NEW APPROACH TO HEALTH AND HEALING

Nobody expects illness, much less long term or serious illness. It is not something that we are brought up to expect and therefore when we are faced with such difficulties we do not have the mental and emotional skills to deal with them effectively or creatively, we have to develop them for ourselves or suffer accordingly.

When we look at the world around us it seems that most people do not get ill or that it only happens to a minority of people and therefore we do not regard it as a realistic worry. This is the way we were brought up and the way our parents were brought up. We learned from them consciously and sub-consciously that there was little need to prepare for something that probably would not occur. Perhaps the most bizarre aspect of this 'head in the sand' philosophy is our attitude towards death. Again it is not something we think about much, perhaps because it makes us feel uncomfortable, yet finally sickness and death is something that nobody however rich or powerful can avoid, so preparing for these unavoidable eventualities is a wise thing to do.

Sickness and death are perhaps the two greatest difficulties that each of us will face, yet these subjects are not on any school curriculum and it is quite rare to find parents who have made an effort to discuss these subjects openly with their children, usually because the parents themselves do not have the wish to examine these issues. Most of us like a quiet life! We do not want to face these realities and prefer to ignore the facts of life and death. Consequently when we are finally faced with illness and death we are almost helpless.

Perhaps we do not like approaching these subjects because they threaten the 'bubble' of temporary happiness in which most of us live. Yet ironically by being honest and brave enough to face these facts of life we can develop a deeper and greater appreciation, fulfilment and enjoyment of life. In this sense illness can be a great teacher; it makes us acutely aware of our own mortality and impermanence. We are forced to acknowledge the fragility of life and in this way become aware of its preciousness and rare qualities.

Generally we spend our lives going from one thing to the next, birth, childhood, school, relationships, college, career, marriage, children, retirement and death. It is often only in old age that we slow down enough to wonder who we are and what the purpose of a human life may be. Illness can be an opportunity to slow down, a chance to take time out and begin looking at the world and ourselves in a new light.

It is important to realise that in every moment you have the power to change your life forever, simply by changing your mind. What separates someone who deals with long term illness successfully and someone who suffers is simply their state of mind. Your personality, character or state of mind is not written in stone or programmed in to you. It is simply the result of the accumulated habits you have developed in response to different circumstances and experiences since the day you were born, plus the habits we developed in previous lives if you feel this to be true. No one is inherently positive or negative, we all have the powers of discrimination and choice. We can discriminate against unhappiness and choose happiness simply by changing our mind.

We have the power to choose to respond positively or negatively to any situation regardless of our habits or tendencies. Of course if you are very familiar with reacting negatively if you do not make the effort to react positively you will never naturally react positively. Strong effort is the key, if we want to take a walk through some woods we will naturally follow the path that is already there, the path of least resistance. However if someone tells us that this path will lead us over the edge of a cliff we might try to make a new path in a safer direction. Certainly this new path will be slow a first as we have to clear away obstacles and debris but if we walk it daily we will find it easier and easier and eventually it will become the easiest way through the woods! If others see that because of the way we are living we are experiencing a constant source of happiness that is not disturbed by the ups and downs of every day life they will also want to find a new path.

Buddha said that 'illness has many good qualities'! This is true if we can transform what we cannot cure into the path to inner happiness. Often illness dispels pride and helps us develop such qualities as patience and contentment. Serious illness really concentrates the mind, it can certainly make us think more deeply about what we value in life and help us to reassess our priorities, our attitudes and our lifestyle. Of course no one would recommend 'learning from illness' as a path of choice, but there are so many examples of people whose lives have been positively transformed simply by learning to look at themselves and their lives in a new light.

This may seem like a strange philosophy for a therapist or healer to share with their clients when so many people prefer to view illness as something to fight against with all their energy. Unfortunately there are many instances when projecting too much energy at a problem, by being 'blindly' or unrealistically positive, will just make things worse. We have to strike a balance in our approach to health and illness. Be realistic but positive, deal with the day to day reality of being ill but don't rule out miracles. The people who learn to wisely adapt and learn to live with long term illness are living examples of a life well spent, however short. Rare qualities like contentment, self-acceptance, inner calm and compassion towards others' suffering can be developed over time. Such qualities are sometimes hard to find in those who appear to be 'successful' and healthy. Hard times can really bring out the best in us if we are willing to use them to train our mind and transform our outlook.

So we can see that illness is not necessarily a negative force; in fact it can be just the opposite, simply by changing our mind we can transform illness or any adverse condition into a meaningful opportunity to develop our own inner qualities. We never know what life is going to 'throw' at us, but we can be ready for it if we are willing to be flexible, positive and willing to accept difficulties and use them to become more whole and 'healthy' human beings.

This raises the question, what is good health? Is it a healthy body or a healthy mind? Many people would say that it is a balance between the two but if we think deeply about this we can see that good health is simply a state of mind. Some people develop the capacity to be deeply happy and content in the most adverse situations; perhaps these people are healthier in some ways than Olympic athletes! Certainly our inner achievements are ultimately of more value than our external triumphs. Although their value is not as immediately obvious they are a real treasure and if we build on them and strive to develop our inner qualities we will find great peace and contentment in this life and far in to the future. Although material wealth and good health give us a sense of security this is always short lived. Sooner or later these things will be taken from us and certainly at the end of our life we will have to leave them behind. There is no reason why we should not enjoy these short-term pleasures but if we expect them to provide some lasting comfort and protection we will be disappointed. If we are happy within our outlook will be positive whatever our circumstances. If we can share this point of view with patients, clients, friends, family or anyone we meet either directly or just through our good example we are really giving others something of great value. To give this kind of wisdom is the wisest kindness. Being happy is an art that many of us have forgotten, being a good healer often means helping people to rediscover their own natural source of happiness from within.

We all live in a slightly different universe! Obviously animals experience a different world to humans but every human also experiences the 'outside' world in a different way. We have different personal perceptions of the same phenomena caused by having different minds. For example when we are young we may not like curry but as we grow older we may change our mind and stop perceiving curry as a source of pain! We may actually begin to see curry as a great source of pleasure. In this instance we can see that curry has not changed from its own side, it was never inherently good or bad! We can apply this to any phenomena at all, nothing is inherently good or bad, we project these qualities on to objects, people, places, etc and then believe them to be real, as if these objects actually possess good or bad qualities within their make-up. Another good example is when we meet someone for the first time we immediately form an opinion of them, however that first opinion is often proved to be wrong and we may easily grow to dislike or like that person given time.

So what relevance does this have to healing techniques? Well simply this: complementary therapies should help us change our mind, not the world around us, by changing our mind all things change. Our perception of ourself, our environment and others changes completely when we change our mind or when our mind is changed. This tried and tested ancient wisdom for solving all our problems can be summed up in one phrase:

PEACEFUL MIND = PEACEFUL WORLD

As mentioned we will never find lasting happiness by trying to manufacture a perfect world for ourselves. We can try to find the best job, the right partner, the nicest house or the fastest car and for a short time we may find some happiness in these things but if we are honest we know in our hearts that this happiness will come to an end. It is not real happiness and often serves to create more problems than it solves. In fact the amount of pain and unhappiness we experience when we are separated from these things will at the very least be proportionate to the amount of 'attachment' we have for them. There is a strong relationship between 'need' and pain. The more we need someone or something to make us happy the more pain we will experience when we are eventually parted from them.

We also spend much time and effort manipulating our world to get what we want, when we want it, when all the happiness and peace of mind we could wish for is literally under our noses! As mentioned if we have a deeply happy mind we can experience all manner of difficult circumstances and unpleasant situations and not feel any less happy. Also we know that if we are deeply unhappy no amount of money, possessions or relationships can help us. So again this shows us that happiness depends upon the mind, not on external factors. Understanding this simple wisdom and taking it to heart should give us great hope because this realisation is the root of great happiness and the essence of a true spiritual path. Many people believe that the door of the mind is the gateway to heaven!

Learning to open our hearts and minds and develop some simple wisdom and contentment is time well spent and the rewards for accumulating these inner treasures are fathomless. This is not some difficult or mystical task, it is very simple and natural to all of us and we can use complementary therapies to help us begin and complete this journey towards self-understanding and lasting peace of mind.

To walk a path of spiritual or personal growth does not mean we have to shave our heads and run to the hills! This would be another extreme and another way of trying to manipulate our world to avoid what we dislike. The real spiritual practitioner realises that they have exactly the right conditions at present to start developing higher qualities within themselves. Whether we are rich or poor does not matter, what matters is that we make an effort to change from within. Simply by making a daily determination to be a little more tolerant, patient, kind and helpful is a great step forward. Then if we can carry forward these determinations in to our daily activities and remind ourselves of our good intentions especially when we are challenged by our own impatience or selfishness then we will begin to make real progress. Just being in the presence of a healer with a little wisdom and compassion is really of more benefit in the long term than a thousand hands-on treatments from some one who is in it for the money, recognition or some other wrong motivation.

Intention and motivation is the key to success, if our motives are good, even if we make a few mistakes, the results will be beneficial right from our very first treatment. It also useful to remember that there is a right and a wrong time for giving advice. When people are not ready to change their minds and move towards good health then bombarding them with well-intentioned advice can be a real turn off, we all know this! So wisdom dictates that a gentle approach, patience and a good listening ear need to be employed until a patient naturally seeks knowledge for a new perspective on an old problem.

We have to also be careful that a sense of wisdom does not breed arrogance or some subtle sense of superiority. Some eastern philosophies teach that the best healers are those that always regard the welfare of others, especially their patients, as most important. This sense of humility, that many of the great spiritual teachers like Jesus and Buddha displayed, is a very rare and great quality. It really allows us to get close to others and helps them to feel comfortable with us. A sense of superiority is a real barrier to the development of any healing relationship.

KARMA - ACTIONS AND THEIR EFFECTS

Basically we can say that any disease, disorder or unhappiness is the result of some disharmony in the body, mind or environment. However it is not an easy task to establish the original cause of a particular problem. From Buddhism we know that the root causes of all our major and minor problems are our own previous negative actions of body, speech and mind returning to us as illness, poverty, ignorance or any other type of unpleasant experience. The word karma directly translates as 'action', what we intentionally create mentally, verbally and/or physically. The laws of karma teach that whatever we create or give out comes back to us sooner or later, just like a boomerang! These negative actions may have been performed many lifetimes ago and it is only now that we might be experiencing the effects or repercussions. We may think that we would never have committed serious negative actions like harming others but in each of our previous lives we were almost completely different to the kind of person we are now. If we met ourselves from a previous life we would not recognise ourselves at all, it would be like meeting a complete stranger.

Buddhism suggests that each lifetime we are almost born anew. On the surface we have completely different bodies and personalities, yet deep within our very subtle mind, soul or higher self we carry the memories, tendencies and imprints of all our previous lives. When the conditions are right our previous actions of body, speech and mind will return to us as positive or negative experiences depending on whether they were well intentioned and beneficial or otherwise. So from a Buddhist perspective to fully heal and prevent future illness we must remove the root causes, or the seeds of our past negative actions from deep within the mind, before they ripen as unpleasant experiences.

We could just as easily say that any person is simply the results of their previous actions ripening as pleasant or unpleasant characteristics and experiences. However because one person is experiencing happiness and good fortune does not necessarily mean they are superior than others or that they have been kinder or more giving in previous lives. We all have an infinite amount of accumulated karma because we have had countless previous lives. We have all been good and bad people in previous lives so we don't know what karma will ripen next, it might be pleasant, it might not.

Unfortunately karma ripens haphazardly, there is no grand plan or great scheme, life is simply a 'karmic lottery', if the conditions are right any sort of karma could ripen, anything could happen to us. We know this is a fact of life; bad things can happen to good people and visa versa. A murderer can be reborn as a king in his next life if he has the karma from a previous life for that to happen, he may experience many fortunate rebirths in wealthy and loving families until eventually the karma of murdering catches up with him. Fortunately we can protect ourselves from our own karma by completely purifying it before it ripens; there is an element of karmic purification, through confession, prayer and meditation, in all religions.

LIBERATION THROUGH ACCEPTANCE

Sometimes no matter how hard we try and no matter what therapies or remedies we use we cannot escape or remove the effects of heavy negative karma that might be ripening in the form of a serious, possibly life-threatening, illness. This is a fact of life that can be difficult to accept. Of course we can use therapies to help us deal with such challenging situations but we also have to be realistic and mature. Sometimes we simply have to accept what is happening to us and stop fighting. Developing a peaceful and happy mind is possible even in the face of great hardship. Learning to accept the things we cannot change and developing compassion for others who may be feeling for us shows great wisdom and maturity. Also accepting difficulties with a peaceful and patient mind actually causes negative karma to be purified and exhausted much more quickly than if we develop anger, frustration or sadness. Of course we may go through these emotions initially on the path to acceptance but if we 'stay there' too long we are only making a difficult situation worse for ourselves and for those we love.

As mentioned Buddhism explains that any illness, before manifesting on the physical or conscious level, initially arises from the very subtle or deepest levels of mind, which are presently sub-conscious to most people. Buddhism explains that we can only remove the true causes of illness by purifying our very subtle mind of all the potential seeds of illness planted or created by our own past negative actions in previous lives.

Even when these seeds have ripened or been removed the mental imprints of these past actions still remain in the mind, like footprints in the sand, and these create the mental tendencies to walk the same path again or commit similar negative actions in the future. These imprints must also be removed if we want to fully prevent illness or other negative experiences coming our way in this and future lives. We can do this by completely purifying our very subtle mind and developing a special type of wisdom, 'liberation' or understanding the true nature of reality or in other words gaining 'enlightenment'. Again this is not some far off unattainable spiritual goal, the potential for us to achieve this is in our very nature, we just need someone to point us the right direction! One tried and tested way toward enlightenment is through practising the simple and clear meditation techniques that Buddha taught. We do not have to become Buddhist to learn these, they are open and available to anyone and they are ideally suited to our needs whatever our circumstances and commitments. In fact we do not need to change our lifestyle at all, only our mind! (See Appendix 1)

THE SOURCE OF ALL SUFFERING

As explained, the main cause of illness is negative karma ripening when the correct conditions are in place. But what causes us to create negative karma? The simple answer to this is that 'our selfish mind causes us to create negative karma'. Likewise a selfless mind causes us to create positive karma that will come back to us as pleasant experiences in the future and then through the power of familiarity, we will also find it easier to repeat this tendency to be kind, thoughtful and selfless again and again, bringing greater and greater good fortune and happiness.

Thinking of the welfare of others is a great source of future happiness and thinking of our own welfare is a source of future suffering. Even in the short term transferring our attention towards others and working for their benefit can take our mind off our own problems and cause us to be less introverted and self-obsessed. The more we worry about a problem the bigger it gets but the more we concern ourselves with helping others the less energy and time we give to our own worries and the weaker and less demanding they become.

We can use this line of reasoning in many practical ways. For example if we have to give a public talk on a particular subject we may be very worried or frightened, especially if we have little experience. But if we change our mind and instead of giving our attention to our own worry, instead think, 'How can I help these people? What can I give them?' then by strongly concentrating on these thoughts our own worries will naturally diminish. This line of reasoning is very powerful and can be applied to many situations that cause us unhappiness or worry.

One of our greatest sources of happiness and unhappiness is relationships and again simply by consistently concentrating on the welfare of the other person in a relationship this will definitely help us to become more content and less demanding or controlling. All the great spiritual teachers have taught and encouraged this; they know that the source of all happiness is caring for others, all others, equally.

Putting others first does not mean we have to be hard on ourselves. On the contrary if we understand and accept the laws of karma we can gain great personal satisfaction from knowing that selfless actions not only benefit others but will also cause us to experience good fortune in the future.

The main factor in creating karma is our true intention or motivation. Many people might appear to be altruistic on the outside, always doing good turns for others, but if their motivation is selfish, perhaps because they want others to like them, then this will not create a good Karmic 'return' in the future. Conversely leading a very normal life with a pure motivation will lead to great future happiness.

So we can say that illness arises from negative karma that was created by selfish actions in a previous life, but what causes us to perform selfish actions, what causes us to think and act in a selfish way? If we can understand the answer to this then we are truly on the way to solving all our problems and finding a lasting cure to any present or potential future illness.

THE UNIVERSAL CURE

We act instinctively and naturally to benefit ourselves because we think we are more important than others. Our sense of 'self' is very dear to us and we cherish it deeply and in many subtle ways. We do not realise how deeply we cherish ourselves until we are faced with situations that frighten or challenge our sense of 'self'. So we have a strong sense of self, a strong sense that we truly exist and that this 'self' is the most important thing in the universe. The fact that we grasp at this sense of 'self', ego or 'I' and believe it to truly exist is the source of all our present and future problems. If we could realise our true nature and abandon the inner ignorance or lack of inner clarity/wisdom that gives rise to the sense of a very important 'self' we could solve all our problems and experience complete and lasting happiness and freedom from suffering forever. Again this may sound unrealistic, unattainable or even bizarre! But this message usually strikes a chord even in the most cynical heart.

We can compare the mind to a glass of sparkling water, the constant stream of bubbles floating to the surface are like our thoughts and feelings. It appears that we 'are' these thoughts and emotions that arise from within, as if they make up our identity and character or as if they are the 'real me'. Our true nature is more like the water itself than the bubbles that arise in it, our essence or source in reality is closer to the space between our thoughts and feelings. Ultimately this inner realisation can become the universal cure for all illness and suffering.

So having established a universal cure for all ills, how do we take it! How can we free ourselves and others from the effects of illness and the potential for future illness and all forms of suffering? The old biblical saying of 'Physician heal thyself' is very relevant here. We cannot truly help others until we have healed ourselves and a true healing is one that is complete and lasting and comes from within. Again we can only accomplish this by realising our true nature and becoming all that we can be, then we will have the wisdom and power to help others achieve the same state of complete happiness and permanent freedom from any kind of problem or unhappiness. To reach this special destination we have to find a clear and authentic spiritual path.

Buddha taught such a path thousands of years ago. Many people received his teachings and found great happiness and inner peace as a result. Because we have an unbroken and pure lineage of these teachings and instructions many people from all backgrounds and religions today are also finding this timeless wisdom invaluable and completely relevant to the problems they face. Ultimately Buddhism is really 'Truism'; if you ever wanted to know who you are, why you're here or just how to be happy, simply pick up a good book on Buddhism! It will be a map of reality.

Having said that, Buddhism does not have a monopoly on the truth, many of Buddha's teachings are reflected in all of the great world religions and spiritual paths to truth and happiness. We cannot say that one is superior or better than another, they all have good qualities and perhaps we can say that they are all leading in a similar direction and come from the same source. As individuals we have to find one that we feel comfortable with and one that we feel shines with clarity and truth.

Working towards and realising our true nature is not a painful or monumental task; we all have the potential and right conditions to achieve spiritual enlightenment in one lifetime. It is said that it is easier to gain enlightenment than it is to achieve a human rebirth, so we have already done most of the work! If we miss this precious opportunity it may not come around again for a long time.

THE MOST EFFECTIVE HEALER

The mind is quite a subtle object and the effects of the thoughts and intentions that accompany our actions are not easily revealed unless we are familiar with our inner world. However we can prove this in another way. If someone were to practice healing and they were in a very negative frame of mind, perhaps impatient or distracted and not that bothered about the welfare of the person they were treating, then this would obviously have a profound effect on the treatment. The client would sense this and not be at ease and leave with little faith in the treatment. So we can see that many 'doors' are already closing and the chance of a successful treatment is reduced. Conversely if the therapist has his or her client's best interests at heart and has a mind of great compassion then this will naturally lead to a successful treatment and also give the client confidence in the therapist and therefore the treatment.

We also have to look again at karma to gain some clarity on this. Obviously the karma of the client and therapist is the key factor in the possibility of a successful treatment. There are two conditions that they can establish that will help the karma of a successful treatment to ripen. From the therapist's side the mind of compassion is important and from the patient's side the minds of patience, faith in the therapist, therapy or the healing 'energy' and the wish to be well are also important. Even if we only have a little of these qualities then that will give the treatment enough 'room' to work well!

Also if the patient themselves can try to develop more compassion for others this will aid their own healing process. A wish to use your life well and help others whenever possible will help the karma of good health to ripen. It is important to stress that this is not a guarantee of good health, many compassionate people suffer from illness, it is simply another 'condition' that can help improve health.

Whatever conditions we create, good and bad karma can only ripen if we have created the causes by planting the seeds of this karma by our actions of body, speech and mind in previous lives. This is why some very negative people never get ill and have long lives and why some very positive people get ill and sometimes die young. It is all about causes and conditions, if we have not created the causes to experience a certain illness or we have removed them through inner purification, whatever conditions we create we will not become ill.

There is one more advantage in trying to develop our compassion, if selfish actions lead to future suffering then compassion must lead to great health and happiness in the future.

FINAL THOUGHTS

There is no substitute for practice if you want to become an accomplished healer. Start practicing on people you know as soon as possible. Try to keep a relaxed peaceful and positive mind while you are treating others and keep an open mind to what might be possible in terms of healing. If the right conditions are present wonderful results can arise. The power of touch is so often underestimated; many people have had the experience of feeling better just by being touched or even just being in the presence of a compassionate person. We can learn all the natural healing techniques you can name but if we do not know how to develop a kind and compassionate mind we will not be much use to others in the long run. Our thoughts and words and actions have an effect on the world around us in both obvious and more subtle ways and it is our responsibility, particularly as a healer, to set a good example and try to make the world a better place by trying to be a better person every day. Again one of the best things we can do is just to cultivate a relaxed, content, positive and kind attitude. Such an approach to life can help us deal with difficult situations more easily and it is a great thing to be able to share this with others when we have some experience. Sometimes it can be tough to change the habits of a lifetime especially if those around don't appreciate or support what we are trying to do, but like anything that is worth fighting for we have to apply much time and thought and effort to gain lasting results. Just remember that everybody wants to be happy and happiness comes from within so all we need to do is gradually let go of looking for happiness from outside and steadily start to rely on a peaceful and happy mind. Then over time we will become a healer in the truest sense of the word.

Medicine Buddha: The embodiment of the healing power of all enlightened beings.

INDEX

APPENDICES

APPENDIX 1 – MEDITATION

APPENDIX 2 – BOOKS ON BUDDHISM

APPENDIX 3 – OTHER THERAPIES AND USEFUL ADDRESSES

APPENDIX 4 – TRADITIONAL CHINESE MEDICINE

APPENDIX 1

MEDITATION

The demand for a lasting solution to the problems of stress and anxiety, created by the nature of today's 'material' society, has led to the setting up of meditation groups in almost every town and city. These groups vary in content and in their spiritual origin, so it is important to find one that you feel comfortable with, one that is run by a fully qualified teacher and one that teaches a recognised and correct 'path' true to the origins of meditation.

BUDDHIST MEDITATION

Most meditation groups can trace their origins back to Buddha, who lived over 2000 years ago. He was born into one of the richest and most powerful royal families in India and spent the first twenty-nine years of his life living as a prince. However, despite having all the health, wealth and good relationships he could wish for he still felt incomplete and he could also see a great need in others for a real solution to life's problems. Finally he came to understand that most people look for happiness in the wrong place! He felt sure that true, lasting, happiness could be found simply by understanding and developing the mind. He decided to give up his inheritance and devote the rest of his life to attaining the ultimate state of wisdom and happiness, so that he could share this with others. All Buddha's teachings were recorded and passed down and to this day we have a pure, unbroken lineage of the path to full enlightenment. This lineage is now firmly established in the West. We do not have to travel far to find it!

NEW KADAMPA TRADITION

One of the largest international Buddhist organisations is the New Kadampa Tradition. Established in 1976 by Tibetan meditation master, Geshe Kelsang Gyatso Rinpoche, its purpose is "to present the mainstream of Buddhist teachings in a way that is relevant and immediately applicable to the contemporary Western way of life". Most cities and towns in the UK have an NKT residential centre or meditation group and many are opening in the US, Europe and all over the world, (see Appendix 2 for books by Geshe Kelsang Gyatso on Buddhism and Buddhist practice). To find your nearest Buddhist centre, or if you would like a teacher to give an introductory talk on Buddhism in your area, please contact:

NEW KADAMPA TRADITION
Manjushri Kadampa Meditation Centre
Conishead Priory
Ulverston
Cumbria
LA12 9QQ
ENGLAND

TEL/FAX: 01229 588533 (within UK)
Email: info@kadampa.org
www.kadampa.org

US CONTACT:
New Kadampa Tradition
Kadampa Meditation Center of America

42 Sweeney Road

Glen Spey NY 12737, USA

Tel: (845) 856-9000

Toll free: 1-877-KADAMPA

fax: (845) 856-2110

e-mail: info@kadampacenter.org

APPENDIX 2

BOOKS ON BUDDHISM

The following books, written by Geshe Kelsang Gyatso and published by Tharpa Publications, provide a practical and inspiring introduction to the Buddhist way of life:

Transform Your Life – A Blissful Journey

Introduction to Buddhism – An Explanation of the Buddhist Way of Life

The New Meditation Handbook – A Practical Guide to Meditation

Universal Compassion – Transforming Your Life Through Love and Compassion

Eight Steps to Happiness – Transform Your Mind, Transform Your Life

How to Solve Our Human Problems – The Four Noble Truths

There are many other more advanced and in depth titles on Buddhism available from Tharpa Publications; they also produce Buddhist art, prayers, CD's, talking books, and books in Braille. For more information visit www.tharpa.com

APPENDIX 3

OTHER THERAPIES AND USEFUL ADDRESSES

Aromatherapy
Aromatheray Resource
www.aworldofaromatherapy.com
Aromatheray Resource
www.aromaweb.com
Aromatherapy Consortium
www.aromatherapy-regulation.org.uk
International Federation of Aromatherapists
www.ifaroma.org
The National Association for Holistic Aromatherapy
www.naha.org
Aromatherapy Trade Council
www.a-t-c.org.uk
The AOC
www.aromatherapy-uk.org
Aromatherapy & Allied Practitioners Association
www.AAPA.org.uk

Bach Flower Remedies
Dr Edward Bach Centre
www.bachcentre.com
Original Bach Flower Essences - www.BachFlower.com
www.bachflower.com
Bach flower research programme - learning about the Bach flower

www.edwardbach.org

Findhorn Flower Essences

www.findhornessences.com

Bach Flower Remedies

www.bachfloweressences.co.uk

Australian Bush Flower Essences

www.ausflowers.com.au

British Association of Flower Essence Producers

www.bafep.com

Flower Remedies Vibrational Essences - The World Wide Essence Society

www.essences.com

Himalayan Flower Enhancers

www.himalaya.com.au

Crystal Therapy

Crystal Healing Resource

www.mindstones.com

International Association of Crystal Healing

www.iacht.co.uk

Crystal Healing Associations

www.crystal-healing.org

Crystal Healing Resource

www.crystalwellbeing.co.uk

Crystal Healing Resource

www.crystaltherapy.co.uk

Herbal Medicine

Herbal Medicine Resource

www.herbalremediesinfo.com

British Herbal Medicine Association

www.bhma.info

British Naturopathic Association

www.naturopaths.org.uk

Chinese Medicine Resource

www.aworldofchinesemedicine.com

Register of Chinese Herbal Medicine

www.rchm.co.uk

Homeopathy

Homeopathic Resource

www.abchomeopathy.com

Homeopathic Resource

www.homeopathic.org

British Homeopathic Association

www.trusthomeopathy.org

Society of Homeopaths

www.homeopathy-soh.org

Homeopathic Resource

www.homeopathyhome.com

North American Society of Homeopaths

www.homeopathy.org

Homeopaththic Resource

www.webhomeopath.com

Meditation

Find a meditation class - anywhere in the world

www.kadampa.org

Books on meditation

www.tharpa.com

Buddhist Hotel in Italy

www.kmcitaly.org

Buddhist Hotel in Spain

www.hotelkadampaspain.com

Buddhist Centre in Cumbria UK

www.manjushri.org

Buddhist Centre Nr. Derby UK

www.taracentre.org.uk

Buddhist Centre in W. Yorkshire UK

www.losangdragpa.com

Buddhist Centre in E. Yorkshire UK

www.madhyamaka.org

Buddhist Centre in Midlands UK

www.meditation-nagarjuna.org

Buddhist Centre in London UK

www.meditateinlondon.org.uk

Buddhist Centre in London UK

www.meditateinwimbledon.org

Buddhist Centre in New York USA

www.kadampanyc.org

Buddhist Centre in New York USA

www.kadampacenter.org

Reflexology

The Association of Reflexologists
www.reflexology.org
British Reflexology Association
www.britreflex.co.uk
International Institute of Reflexology (UK)
www.reflexology-uk.co.uk
Reflexology Research
www.reflexology-research.com
Advanced Reflexology Training
www.artreflex.com
Reflexology Association of America
www.reflexology-usa.org
International Institute of Reflexology
www.reflexology-usa.net
International Academy of Advanced Reflexology
www.reflexology.net
Modern Institute of Reflexology
www.reflexologyinstitute.com
International Reflexology Directory USA
www.internationalholistictherapiesdirectories.com

Reiki

The Reiki Association
www.reikiassociation.org.uk
UK Reiki Federation
www.reikifed.co.uk
Reiki Evolution

www.reiki-evolution.co.uk

The International Center for Reiki Training

www.reiki.org

Reiki Dharma

www.reikidharma.com

Usuido

www.usui-do.org

Yoga

Yoga Resource

www.abc-of-yoga.com

Yoga Resource

www.yogabasics.com

British Wheel of Yoga

www.bwy.org.uk

Yoga Resource

www.yoga.co.uk

American Yoga Association

www.americanyogaassociation.org

International Association of Yoga Therapists

www.iayt.org

Yoga Alliance

www.yogaalliance.com

British Wheel of Yoga

www.bwy.org.uk

International Yoga Federation

fiy.yoganet.org

Yoga Magazine

www.yogajournal.com

Yoga Magazine

www.yogamagazine.co.uk

Other Useful Websites

British Accupuncture Council

www.acupuncture.org.uk

British Medical Acupuncture Society

www.medical-acupuncture.co.uk

Alexander Technique

www.stat.org.uk

www.alexandertechnique.com

General Health

www.mercola.com

Ayurveda

www.ayurveda.com

British Naturopathic Association

www.naturopaths.org.uk

Bowen Technique

www.thebowentechnique.com

Hypnotherapy

www.thehypnotherapyassociation.co.uk

Iridology

www.gni-international.org

Kinesiology

www.kinesiologyfederation.org

Nutrition

www.nutrition.org.uk

Oesteopathy

www.osteopathy.org.uk

Shiatsu

www.shiatsu.org

Massage

www.massagetherapy.co.uk

Complementary Therapies

www.rccm.org.uk

The British Complementary Medicine Association

www.bcma.co.uk

Bristol Cancer Help Centre

www.bristolcancerhelp.org.uk

The Institute for Complementary Medicine

www.icmedicine.co.uk

The Prince of Wales's Foundation of Integrated Health

www.fihealth.org.uk

National Centre for Complementary and Alternative Medicine

www.nccam.nih.gov

British Holistic Medical Association

www.bhma.org

British Medical Association

bma.org.uk

British Register for Complimentary Practitioners

www.i-c-m.org.uk

Guild of Complimentary practitioners

www.gcpnet.com

Health Professions Council

www.hpc-uk.org

APPENDIX 4

TRADITIONAL CHINESE MEDICINE

We do not need to have an understanding of Chinese medicine to be a good healer but it can help us to develop a more holistic understanding of complementary therapies. It is recommended that the reader seek appropriate training before applying any of this knowledge in practice. Chinese medicine is based on the principles of internal balance and harmony, this highly refined and complex discipline works to regenerate the body's organs and systems. Each human is viewed as a mini-ecosystem that shares common traits with the earth on which we live.

The Chinese have a concept of vital energy known as chi or qi (pronounced chee), which is the basis of all life. In the body, chi is transported via the 12 major energetic pathways known as meridians. Although these meridians cannot be seen with the naked eye, modern science has proven their existence through electronic detection. Each meridian connects to one of the major organs, and chi is said to power the organ, enabling effective functioning. For example, the path of the heart meridian travels from the heart, to the armpit, and down the inside of the arm to the little finger. This explains why some individuals with heart conditions will express a tingling feeling running down the arm and into the fingers. Chi is regulated by the forces of yin and yang.

The Chinese symbol for Yin literally means "the dark side of the mountain", and represents the qualities of cold, still, dark, below, weakness, and void. The Chinese symbol for yang translates to "the sunny side of the mountain", and therefore represents the opposite qualities of Yin: heat, activity, light, above, strength, and solidity. A person's constitution, or the nature of the disease is determined by the aspects of yin and yang. Harmony and balance of this union yields a healthy state, whereas excess or deficiency of either yin or yang is thought to lead to illness.

The basic principles of this complete medical system can be explained in seven sections: Causes of Disharmony, Meridians, Five Elements, Vital Substances, yin and yang, Zangfu, Diagnosis.

1 CAUSES OF DISHARMONY

Traditional Chinese Medicine views the cause of disease in three main areas: external causes, internal causes, and a group of miscellaneous causes, which primarily involve lifestyle.

THE SIX EXTERNAL CAUSES

The six external causes of disease, also known as the six evils, are causes of disharmony that relate to climatic conditions. Just as extremes of wind, cold, heat, dampness, dryness, and summer heat can have devastating effects on the world in which we live, they can also seriously alter the balance within the body by diminishing, or blocking the flow of chi in the organs.

Wind is the most prevalent of the six external factors, and refers to the ability of an illness to spread within the body. Symptoms commonly linked with wind include chills, fever, colds, flu, nasal congestion, headaches, allergies, arthritic and rheumatic conditions, as well as dizziness and vertigo.

Cold related imbalances manifest as conditions that diminish the body's immune system, such as colds, coughs, upper respiratory allergies, as well as poor circulation, anaemia, and weak digestion.

Heat conditions are described as hot and inflammatory, exacerbated by hot weather and exposure to direct heat. They represent an over-active metabolic process, which can result in hypertension, hyperthyroid, ulcers, colitis, inflamed arthritic joints, as well as flu and skin rashes.

Dampness symptoms are created through the intake of oily and fluidic foods, as well as wet weather. These symptoms may include swelling, obesity, the formation of cysts, tumours, and lumps, and an increased production of phlegm. This phlegm production can affect the sinuses and upper respiratory passages, including the lungs and bronchioles.

Dryness can damage vegetation, and creates similar imbalances within the body, causing disorders of the lungs, sinuses, large intestine, skin, digestion, and reproductive organs.

Summer Heat, or an overexposure to sunlight and hot weather, can yield conditions such as heat stroke, dizziness, nausea, extreme thirst, and exhaustion.

THE SEVEN INTERNAL CAUSES

The seven internal causes, otherwise known as the Seven Emotions, are illnesses brought about by intense, prolonged, or suppressed feelings, and are defined as follows:

Sadness decreases the flow of chi in the lungs and heart, and is associated with depression, fatigue, shortness of breath, asthma, allergies, cold and flu.

Grief is similar to sadness, and injures the lungs, decreases immunity to colds and flu, as well as chronic upper respiratory diseases such as emphysema, allergies, and asthma.

Pensiveness, or over-engaging the mind in activities such as worry, thought, or study can deplete spleen chi, and may result in oedema, digestive disorders, low appetite, and fatigue.

Fear or paranoia causes chi to descend, resulting in potential harm to the kidneys, lower back, or joints when this emotion is ever present.

Fright or shock is unlike fear in the sense that the onset is very sudden, causing one's chi to diverge. The rapid change in flow first affects the heart in symptoms such as breathlessness and palpitations, then moves to the lower body in a similar fashion to fear, damaging the kidneys, lower back, and joints.

Anger encompasses all the negative emotions of rage, irritability, frustration, and resentment, and causes the chi to rise inappropriately. Anger is associated with headaches, mental confusion, dizziness, and hypertension.

Joy in Chinese Medicine refers to excess, or overabundance, and relates to illness relative to overindulgence. Damage to the heart may result, and the conditions of hysteria, muddled thought, and insomnia may arise.

2 THE MERIDIAN SYSTEM

In addition to chi, Traditional Chinese Medicine recognizes a subtle energy system by which chi is circulated through the body. This transportation system is referred to as the channels or meridians. There are twelve main meridians in the body, six yin and six yang, and each relates to one of the Zangfu, or organs.

To better visualize the concept of chi, and the meridians, think of the meridians as a river-bed, over which water flows and irrigates the land; feeding, nourishing and sustaining the substance through which it flows.

(In Western medicine, the concept would be likened to the blood flowing through the circulatory system.) If a dam were placed at any point along the river, the nourishing effect that the water had on the whole river would stop at the point the dam was placed.

The same is true in relation to chi and the meridians. When chi becomes blocked, the rest of the body that was being nourished by the continuous flow, now suffers. Illness and disease can result if the flow is not restored. <u>Acupuncture</u> is one tool used to restore the flow of chi, by inserting needles into the acupuncture points (located on the meridians). These insertions are said to clear any residing blockages, or dams, thus freeing the river to better feed the body in its entirety.

3 THE FIVE ELEMENTS

The five elements, also called "Wu Xing" represent the processes that are fundamental to the cycles of nature, and therefore correspond to the human body. In relation to the five elements, the cycle of processes can be represented as:

wood feeds fire

fire creates ashes which form earth

inside the earth, metal which is heated liquefies and produces water vapour

water generated then nourishes the trees, or wood

The five elements, their characteristics, and their inter-relationships with the body can be defined as:

Fire: Hot, ascending, light and energy as embodied in the TCM functions of the heart (yin) and small intestine (yang). The fire element also affects the complementary organ processes of the pericardium (yin) and the triple warmer, which is representative of the upper, lower, and middle parts of the body, as well as the circulation of fluids in these areas (yang). Joy (overindulgence) is the emotion which creates imbalance within this element.

Earth: Productive, fertile, growth. The earth element relates to the stomach (yang) and the spleen (yin). The stomach begins the process of digestive breakdown, while the spleen transforms and transports the energy from food and drink throughout the body. Pensiveness is the emotion which creates imbalance within this element.

Metal: As a conductor, this element includes the lungs (yin), which move vital energy throughout the body, and the large intestine (yang), which is responsible for receiving and discharging waste. Sadness or grief is the emotion which creates imbalance within this element.

Water: Wet, descending, flowing. The water element represents the urinary bladder (yang), and the kidney (yin). The bladder receives, stores, and excretes urine. Water metabolism dissipates fluids throughout the body, moistening it, then accumulating in the kidneys. The kidneys also store the essence, and serve as the root of yin and yang for the entire body. Fear and paranoia are the emotions which create imbalance within this element.

Wood: Strong, rooted. The wood element represents the liver (yin), and the gall bladder (yang). The liver stores blood, and regulates the smooth flow of chi. The gallbladder is responsible for storing and excreting bile. Anger is the emotion that creates imbalance within the liver, while indecisiveness is relative to the gallbladder.

VITAL SUBSTANCES

Traditional Chinese Medicine views the human body as a mini eco-system, which therefore shares the same qualities as nature. Just as the earth contains air, water, and land, the basic substances of the human body are chi, body fluids, blood, and essence.

Chi is the vital energy that gives us our capacity to move, think, and feel. It protects from illness, and warms the body. Chi is derived from two main sources: the air we breathe, and the food we eat. When the supply of chi to the body is depleted or blocked, organ function is adversely affected by the inability to transform and transport the "energy" necessary to fight illness and disease.

Body fluids (called Jin Ye) are the liquids which protect, nurture, and lubricate the body in conjunction with the blood. The moisture nourishes the skin, muscles, joints, spine, bone marrow, and brain. Dehydration results in conditions such as dry skin and constipation, while excess fluids manifest in symptoms such as lethargy, and increased production of phlegm.

Blood is the material foundation for bone, nerve, skin, muscle, and organ creation. It also contains the Shen (spirit) which balances the psyche.

Essence, or Jing, is the body's reproductive and regenerative substance. Essence regulates growth, development, reproduction, and promotes and works with chi to help protect the body from external factors.

The vital substances circulate through the pathways, or meridians, linking all parts of the body. When flowing smoothly they contribute to the healthy state, but if these substances are congested or depleted, symptoms as varied as aches, tension, swelling, asthma, indigestion, and fatigue may result from the disruption.

5 YIN AND YANG

In Chinese medicine, health is represented as a balance of yin and yang. These two forces represent the bipolar manifestation of all things in nature, and because of this, one must be present to allow the other to exist. Hence, where there is above there is below, whatever has a front also has a back, night is followed by day, etc. On an emotional level, one would not know joy had they never experienced pain.

It is important to note that the balance of yin and yang is not always exact, even when the body is healthy. Under normal circumstances the balance is in a state of constant change, based on both the external and internal environment.

For example, during times of anger, a person's mood is more fiery, or yang, and yet once the anger has subsided, and a quiet peaceful state is achieved, yin may dominate.

This shift in the balance of yin and yang is very natural. It is when the balance is consistently altered, and one (be it yin or yang) regularly dominates the other, that health is compromised, resulting in illness and disease.

Traditional Chinese Medicine practitioners attempt to determine the exact nature of the imbalance, and then correct it through the use of acupuncture, herbal remedies, exercise, diet and lifestyle. As balance is restored in the body, so is health.

6 ZANGFU

Zangfu is the term used to describe various yin and yang organs in the body. A yin organ is called a Zang, while a yang organ is called a Fu.

Although the organs are identified by their western anatomical names, Traditional Chinese Medicine views their function on a far broader scope, due in part to the concepts of chi, and essence, their flow, and storage responsibilities.

The twelve organs of Chinese medicine, which correspond to the twelve meridians, or channels within the body, are classified according to the functions of transformation (yin organs), or transportation (yang organs). The Zang is made up of the six solid (yin) organs; the heart, pericardium (sac surrounding the heart), lungs, spleen, liver and kidney. The Fu consists of the six hollow (yang) organs; the small intestine, triple warmer (an organ function), stomach, large intestine, gallbladder and the urinary bladder.

7 DIAGNOSIS

The diagnostic process of Chinese medicine involves four areas, known as the Four Examinations, these are:

Observation: of the patient's complexion, eyes, tongue, nails, gait (overall physical appearance), openness, and emotional demeanour.

Listening and Smelling: the focus being on the sound of the voice and breathing, as well as any odours associated with the body, or breath.

Questioning: for information on present and past complaints including appetite, digestion, bowel movement, bladder, sweat, pain, patterns of sleep, family health history, work, living habits, physical environment, and emotional life.

Palpation: or touching the body to determine temperature, moisture, pain or sensitivity, and the taking of the pulse. The Chinese method of pulse taking involves placing three fingers on each wrist to measure a total of 12 pulses, each associated with a corresponding meridian. Fourteen different pulse characteristics (slow, rapid, full, empty, etc.) are compared with each of the 12 pulses, and are used to determine which organ is not working properly.

Treatments aim to adjust and restore the yin/yang balance, and may incorporate one or more therapies including acupuncture, herbal remedies, exercise and diet.

OBSERVATION

The observation portion of diagnosis begins the moment the patient appears before the practitioner. In this step, the practitioner is forming an initial impression of the patient, while assessing the seriousness of the condition based on four main considerations:

Vitality: the colour, complexion and lustre of the skin, and the overall general impression of the patient are key points in observation. The appearance of the face is an excellent indicator of vitality as all the acupuncture meridians flow to the face, by their primary or secondary pathways, and the state of blood and chi is very evident in this area. As well, the colour of the face may reveal problems in the functioning of the organs. For example, black circles under the eyes could indicate kidney weakness, whereas red colouring (which relates to heat/fire) is linked with the heart. Black or blue colouring is linked with the kidneys, blue-green may involve the liver, and white implies a lung problem.

Body Appearance: the appearance of the body can also provide the practitioner with good information as to where the problems lie. At this point the practitioner is mainly looking for the distribution of fat, type of build, appearance of body hair, etc. For example, it is difficult for yang chi to be distributed in a body with excess fat, therefore an overweight person is more susceptible to cardiac arrest and stroke.

Facial Features: facial expressions tell the practitioner about the psychological status of the patient, whether it be sad, happy, anxious or overjoyed, and are a point of consideration prior to making a diagnosis. The features themselves, including the eyes, nose, mouth and lips, can also provide evidence of excess or deficient conditions causing imbalance in the body.

The Tongue and its Coating: the inspection of the tongue is a vital diagnostic procedure in the practice of Traditional Chinese Medicine. The colour, coating, shape and texture of various parts of the tongue yield information about the state of the organs. A normal tongue is moist and has an "appropriate" red colour. A light red or pale tongue is a sign of deficiency in both chi and blood. A thick, purple coloured tongue is often associated with alcoholism, while cracks in the tongue show dryness, heat, and deficient yin. Prior to an examination, it is important not to eat or drink anything that will discolour the tongue and give a misleading impression to the practitioner.

LISTENING AND SMELLING

A significant aspect of this part of diagnosis is the breathing of the patient and the sound of the voice. A loud assertive voice suggests a yang pattern, while a weak or timid voice suggests the opposite, a yin pattern. Restless and heavy breathing occurs in an excess syndrome whereas shallow breathing is indicative of a deficient condition. Even the sound of a cough gives an indication of the level of phlegm in the lungs, and can be loud and sudden or weak and persistent.

The odour of the body and its excretions are also important aids in diagnosis, and require many years of experience to perfect. As such, this method is more widely practiced in traditional eastern diagnosis than it is in the western practices.

In general terms, there are two distinct smells, which are considered to detect the presence of a hot, excess condition from a cold, deficient one. Yang (hot, excess) conditions are associated with a rancid or rotten smell and Yin (cold, deficient) conditions possess a strong, fishy aroma. As a rule, any unusual or abnormal odours can indicate an illness, those listed above are merely a guideline.

QUESTIONING

During the first visit, a considerable amount of time is spent asking the patient for details about his or her general condition. These questions relate to all emotional, physical, and energy related signs and symptoms, and can help the practitioner form a more complete picture of the patient's condition. A full medical history is usually taken, including details of past illness, operations, physical and mental traumas. While these issues may not seem pertinent to the patient at this juncture, they do provide important insights into the pattern of disharmony existing within the patient.

Other important questions which may be asked are:

Preferences for heat or cold

Frequency and consistency of urination and defecation

Sleep patterns

Diet and thirst

Menstrual cycle (length, pain associated, heaviness of bleeding, etc.)

Headaches (when they occur, where and under what circumstances)

Perspiration (amount, time of day, circumstances)

In addition, the practitioner may inquire regarding the nature of any pain or discomfort, as reactions to heat or cold may point to patterns of excess and deficiency, such as imbalances in yin and yang. For example, if pain is relieved by heat, a cold condition (yin) is indicated. If the reverse is true, such as a discomforts alleviated by cold, a yang condition could be present. The site(s) of the pain are also noted as they may indicate a blockage or stagnation of chi within the meridians of the body.

PALPATION

Palpation, or touching, is a form of diagnosis made by feeling and tapping local areas of the body to ascertain:

Painful areas

Temperature of the skin (heat, cold)

Swelling

Perspiration

Colour

Pulse diagnosis, as it applies to Traditional Chinese Medicine, is the most important form of palpation, and is very different from that of Western physicians. In performing pulse palpation, the practitioner places the index, middle, and ring fingers on the radial artery. Three degrees of pressure, the light touch, the medium touch, and the heavy touch are applied to the region and correspond to the upper, middle, and lower areas of the body. In traditional terms, there are 28 pulse classifications, which describe the way the pulse feels to the fingertip. Some examples of these classifications are:

Slippery – feels like a rolling pearl in a basin, very fluid and full

Choppy – has no strength and is irregular

Full – large and rounded, can be felt at all levels

Empty – hard to detect or felt only slightly at the superficial level when pressure is applied

Slow – slower than the normal rate of four to five beats per breath

Rapid – six to seven beats per breath

Superficial – easily felt on the skin surface

Deep – only felt with a heavy touch

These, along with 20 other descriptions, must be taken into consideration during pulse diagnosis. This requires a tremendous amount of skill and practice, and when properly executed is one of the most important and accurate means of correctly diagnosing a patient. In fact, pulse and tongue diagnosis are considered to be the "two pillars" of the four examinations in traditional practice.

Thanks to www.aworldofchinesemedicine.com for providing information for this appendix.

O

is a symbol of the world,
of oneness and unity. O Books
explores the many paths of wholeness
and spiritual understanding which
different traditions have developed down
the ages. It aims to bring this knowledge
in accessible form, to a general readership,
providing practical spirituality to today's seekers.

For the full list of over 200 titles covering:

- CHILDREN'S PRAYER, NOVELTY AND GIFT BOOKS
- CHILDREN'S CHRISTIAN AND SPIRITUALITY
- CHRISTMAS AND EASTER
- RELIGION/PHILOSOPHY
- SCHOOL TITLES
- ANGELS/CHANNELLING
- HEALING/MEDITATION
- SELF-HELP/RELATIONSHIPS
- ASTROLOGY/NUMEROLOGY
- SPIRITUAL ENQUIRY
- CHRISTIANITY, EVANGELICAL
  AND LIBERAL/RADICAL
- CURRENT AFFAIRS
- HISTORY/BIOGRAPHY
- INSPIRATIONAL/DEVOTIONAL
- WORLD RELIGIONS/INTERFAITH
- BIOGRAPHY AND FICTION
- BIBLE AND REFERENCE
- SCIENCE/PSYCHOLOGY

Please visit our website,
www.O-books.net

SOME RECENT O BOOKS

Reiki Mastery
For second degree students and masters
David Vennells
3rd printing
An excellent reference for anyone interested in hands-on healing.
Helpful and insightful, good and solid. **Amazon**
190381670X 192pp **£9.99 $14.95**

Healing Hands
Simple and practical reflexology techniques for developing god health and inner peace
David Vennells
Promising good health and inner peace, this practical guide to reflexology techniques may not be a glossy affair but it is horoughly and clearly illustrated. Hand reflexology isn't as well known as the foot variety, but it's undeniably effective and, perhaps most usefully, it's a technique that can be applied for self-treatment. Whatever the healing process is that you're going through, whenever you're experiencing it, Healing Hands can support your journey. **Wave**
1905047126 192pp **£9.99 $16.95**

Everything is a Blessing
Make your life a little easier, less stressful and more meaningful
David Vennells
Looks to the spiritual traditions of East and West, the path of "others" rather than the path of "self". Lasting personal growth is not achieved by solving problems for our own benefit, but following a more broadminded, spiritual and longer-term approach.
1905047223 160pp **£11.99 $19.95**